THE GIRL
WHO STOLE
MY
HOLOCAUST

THE GIRL
WHO STOLE
MY
HOLOCAUST

Noam Chayut

Translated by Tal Haran

VERSO

London • New York

This English-language edition published by Verso 2013
Translation © Tal Haran 2013
First published as ‏רׁׁׁׅ ‏רׁׁׄ ‏רׁׁׄ
© Am Oved, Tel Aviv, 2010

1 3 5 7 9 10 8 6 4 2

Verso
UK: 6 Meard Street, London W1F 0EG
US: 20 Jay Street, Suite 1010, Brooklyn, NY 11201
www.versobooks.com

Verso is the imprint of New Left Books

ISBN-13: 978-1-78168-088-9

British Library Cataloguing in Publication Data
A catalogue record for this book is available from the British Library

Library of Congress Cataloging-in-Publication Data
A catalog record for this book is available from the Library of Congress

Typeset in Elektra by Hewer Text UK Ltd, Edinburgh
Printed in the US by Maple Vail

In sacred memory of Abir Aramin and Smadar Elhanan

THE GIRL
WHO STOLE
MY
HOLOCAUST

FOREWORD

This book was born of an accident. Let me explain. I traveled to India for my vacation. One of those post-graduation trips. That is the Israeli code name. A good definition for what you do in life helps you place yourself in society. As I sat in a *dhaba*—a cheap Indian restaurant—in the town of Rishikesh, an Israeli girl approached me and posed a question.

"Student?" she asked.

"Yes," I answered. "Actually, I've just graduated."

"Oh," she said. "Then you're on a post-graduation trip. Me and my girlfriend are on the last leg of our post-army trip. It'll soon be a year. How long can we keep going? We've had enough. We're heading home, that's it. How long are you planning to travel? Wow, cool."

And that's how I came upon the definition for this period of my life. From Rishikesh I headed north to Leh, in the Ladakh desert. First of all because I like deserts, and second because of the monsoon season in the south. This is also the ideal time to explore the Ladakhian plain, which is frozen over the rest of the year.

1

Leh is a charming town in the heart of a breathtaking landscape: a green oasis surrounded by an expansive desert. The ground is colorful, with bright yellow, brown, green and red stretching out all the way to the horizon, in fascinating contrast with the distant snowy peaks ornamenting the barren plain.

Leh is beautiful indeed, but it did not welcome me.

At first I suffered altitude sickness—I simply had no air. Three or four days later, as I began to recuperate, some nasty virus attacked my partner and kept her in bed for a whole week, during which time I came down with violent food poisoning that kept me in the guesthouse and on the toilet bowl, tormented with nausea and horrendous belly aches. When we began to recover, we wanted to liven up our convalescence, so we traveled to one of the neighboring villages. There—perhaps because of the bedbugs or for some other reason—my partner developed a rash on her hands and neck that soon spread to her whole body. Still pale from her sick days, she resembled a white sheet with red spots all over it. Another two or three days went by and I, too, developed a rash on my hands, belly and forehead, while my nausea and dizzy spells continued.

When we finally felt better, we decided to try an experience favored by many travelers in that region: descending a mountain road on a bicycle. A Jeep took us up 5,200 meters above sea level, the highest point in the world accessible by road. From there we coasted back down on our bicycles to Leh, about fifty kilometers as the crow flies, and an altitude difference of about 1,700 meters. In the sheer adrenalin rush I lost all sense of responsibility or fear. I left the group far behind and glided among the mountaintops.

I felt the tremendous smile spreading over my face, hurting my cheeks, a smile reserved for skiing or galloping on horseback along the beach. I took one of the curves too fast. There was sand in the middle of the road and my tires skidded. I almost managed to stabilize myself on one side of the road but hit a protruding metal rod. My bicycle toppled over. I was hurled forward and crashed on some rocks. After rolling over once or twice, I found myself sitting on my ass, stunned and barely breathing. I cursed myself for my irresponsible speed, but was also proud of my "parachute landing," which prevented worse injury. Except for some cuts on my knees, left hip and one hand, I found no other injuries. Thinking that the shock of falling had helped sustain my breathing, I returned to the bicycle and continued my ride, even enjoying it, although my breathing difficulties were replaced by a growing pain in my chest. Then it even hurt to sit down and stand up, to bend over and swallow, and especially to cough and yawn. Even the slightest sneeze resulted in pain lasting for minutes. I could only fall asleep on my back or curled up on my right side, but changing positions was torture and the pain woke me up.

A visit to the Ladakh hospital is a depressing experience, but at least my visit was cheap.

I was very glad to have included high-risk sports in my insurance policy. However, since registering for a doctor's appointment cost only two rupees (or twenty agorot—Israeli cents) and the x-ray cost another forty-five, and the medication which I didn't use cost another thirty rupees, all my medical expenses amounted to only seven Israeli shekels and seventy agorot. Even including the taxi fare to and from the hospital, the insurance charges cost less than the stamp for mailing the forms home.

In the x-ray room at the hospital was a woman sprawled in a wheelchair, her whole body badly injured. She had apparently been in a traffic accident. Her face was swollen, eyes shut, and her whole body was badly bruised. Outside, there was some commotion and the entire staff was glued to the window looking out. When I entered, I saw that the woman's IV bag, connected to a vein in her right hand, was on the floor. It must have fallen, I thought. I tapped the shoulder of a white-robed woman and pointed to the IV bag and the connecting hub that was dripping blood. She shooed me away angrily and resumed looking out the window and chatting with her colleagues. I picked up the drip myself and went over to the next bed, tapping the shoulder of another white-robed woman to show her the dripping blood. She too ignored me. Then, when the injured woman was laid on the x-ray table, none of the many patients and staff in the room were required to leave. I was the only one who hurried out before the x-ray was taken. Apparently, the technicians do not understand what repeated radiation doses do to them or their patients. Or perhaps they understand very well and simply shrug, fully prepared to cross over to the next incarnation that awaits their Buddhist souls.

I waited in the corridor, facing the blue European Union flag, with its bright stars a proud reminder of the EU's complacence and generous donations. Even when my turn came to be x-rayed and I was placed with my back to the wall, and the x-ray technician was already approaching the button, no one left the crowded room. I moved aside to prevent the x-ray, gesturing that I needed something to protect my precious testicles. The technician did not understand me so I left the room to look for something myself. In a corner of a side room— some kind of junk-storage space—was a pile of robes that seemed to serve this purpose. I wrapped them around my loins and was so proud of my resourcefulness that I never wondered about the light weight of the robe. When I got out of the room after being x-rayed, I realized I had merely wrapped myself with a synthetic cloth, empty of the lead shield it was supposed to contain.

I discovered that the only way to heal a fractured rib was to rest, and to do nothing else. I considered going back home to Israel and resting at my parents' house, but I concluded that convalescing in India would be almost as enjoyable as hiking there, which had been my original plan. I also discovered that the most relaxed trip I could manage following my injury was amazingly similar to the trips taken by many other backpackers. I began to like the idea of recovering from my injury in India. One Belgian hiker recommended a place in northern India she said would be ideal for my purposes: "Go to Pushkar," she told me.

A painful flight to the capital, a comfortable train ride in luxury class—and there I was. Pushkar is a village in Rajasthan, the largest Indian state by area, located in the northwest of the country. Pushkar is on nearly every Israeli backpacker's itinerary. The food is tasty, accommodations are comfortable, and both are remarkably cheap. The village itself is quaint and picturesque. But the truth is I am not good at resting. After two days of reading and visits to Hindu temples and short slow walks around the lake, I was getting bored with resting.

On the third day, while taking a hot morning shower, I had an epiphany. This will surely sound a bit florid but I know no other way of describing it: she came to me in a flash — the girl who stole my Holocaust. I saw her face clearly in my mind, that girl from my past. But it was not just a recollection; I also finally deciphered her real meaning in my life. So what might have otherwise been a traumatic memory actually filled me with bliss, for I knew I had an idea: a project was conceived. Sparing my fractured ribs, I held back a burst of joyful laughter and got out of the shower infused with energy and fresh power.

I dressed right away, picked up a notebook and pen and walked over to the nearest *dhaba*. I ordered a banana lassi — banana yoghurt full of surprises, like coconut, raisins and cashews — and began to write and write and write.

Writing, I discovered, made me happy the way I had been in my youth when I took theater workshops or performed music in public. Many of the reminiscences I committed to paper were harsh, but writing them down produced a sweet sense of relief. Although I had recounted these tales many times before, committing them to paper in my fresh, focused frame of mind was immensely pleasing and generated profound, unexpected insights. And so my imposed rest yielded these notes. They quickly became the true purpose of my trip to India. Every four or five days I would move to another beautiful place and walk around a bit or rent a scooter to briefly acquaint myself with the area. But every day at dawn and again at dusk I would sit down and enjoy throwing myself into writing.

Before my epiphany, I was often asked about the moment that transformed me, when I realized that something in me was wrong—the moment when my mind quaked. I used to answer that there was no such moment, no instant of enlightenment. It is a gradual emotional process, I would say, deep and long and full of fragmented realization. But that morning, on a beach ornamented with coconut trees, I had a new answer—this book is the answer to just that question. There was indeed such a moment, but it only became clear to me years after it happened.

October 2007, Varkala Beach, Kerala, India

PART ONE

CHAPTER 1

I mustn't be this sad. It's just a Holocaust. My Holocaust. After all, there are many other things worth living for, such as love and the simple pleasure of existence. Not everyone has a Holocaust. Or even had one at some point. Here, these two Indian women sitting across from me in the restaurant with their huge platter of fruit, yoghurt and honey drops, they never had a Holocaust. And I got mine by birthright, never had to do a thing to earn it. So it would not be fair for me to mourn its loss. And still it hurts, losing my Holocaust. It hurts so very much. Glory snatched from me after a mere twenty-three years of life. How could I not be sorry? Some of my best friends and acquaintances still hold on to theirs. Why have I, of all people, been left without a Holocaust of my own?

Clearly I must introduce my Holocaust to you so that you can understand the splendor of which I was robbed. I must also share with you the story of its theft, for otherwise you won't know how a Holocaust is stolen, will you? And while doing this I will also tell you about the thief herself. My encounter with the girl who stole my Holocaust is not at all a simple chain of events. For you to understand it, I will have to tell you how I happened to be led into that small village behind the lines—borders, but especially dividing lines of culture, logic and sanity—the village where this natural possession of my Holocaust was so forcefully taken away from me.

CHAPTER 2

I wonder whether any man, inspired by the sweet sadness of a Holocaust memorial ceremony, has ever proposed to a woman. I did. I proposed friendship. I swear! "Want to be my girl-friend?" I asked a pretty girl, the prettiest in our group, at the end of the Holocaust Memorial ceremony at our *moshav.*[*] I had an erection, my first as far as I can remember; it was perhaps the first thrill I experienced relating to the opposite sex. I was in the fourth grade and cried at the ceremony. I cried with pride, as I did at all the Holocaust Memorials of my child-hood. I sat next to her and she cried, too, her cheeks chubby, red and wet with enticing tears. That's Holocaust Memorial Day: everyone gets serious, wears a deep and concentrated look and cries together, mourning the "splendor of youth and glory of courage. Do not forget, do not forgive."[†]

On the eve of Holocaust Memorial Day we would walk together, my father, mother, brother and sisters, to the

---

[*] A community of farmers.

[†] From the prayer opening the ceremony.

community hall in the middle of our village. It was a huge building. One can hardly imagine how awesome and powerful it looked, especially to a young child. This feeling of awe prevailed not only during Holocaust commemorations, but also during "*moshav* festivities," marking the founding of the village. The *moshav* celebration was originally held during the Hanukka holidays, but eventually the date was changed to coincide with *Shavuot*.* Over the years the celebration also moved outside the building, to the nearby football field.

In the winter of 1921—December 16 to be exact—the soon-to-be founders of the village where I was born loaded their wagons, harnessed them to mules and headed east towards Harod Stream. From there they crossed the gentle slopes above Tabun Spring. The animals strained at their harnesses, struggling with the muddy loam of the Jezre'el Valley, lands that had been freshly purchased and not yet drenched in blood. Toward evening, the pioneers climbed the hill where the village is now located and pitched their first tents just before the Hanukka holidays.

But the date itself was not sanctified and the *moshav* festivities were eventually combined with the celebration of *Shavuot*. This was done because *Shavuot* draws the energies of farmers past and present and of the community at large to hail the changing seasons, the bounty of the earth, and—perhaps not quite consciously—the granting of the Torah, whether or not

---

* Traditionally, the day celebrating both the first harvest of the summer and the Jewish people's receiving the Torah.

the last of these actually took place. Doubtless its power has preserved this special date through two thousand years of exile.

The community hall was also where we celebrated simpler holidays. The youth movement used it to celebrate Hanukka, Purim and Tu Bishvat. The hall had a loft called "The Members' Club" that was shrouded in mystery. Nowadays, with our culture so Americanized, we Israelis are somewhat amused to recall that the word *chaver** had socialist or even communist undertones — "member of the *moshav* association." As a child, I took it quite literally. However, the shouts that emanated from that club, the curses and profanities voiced by people coming out and passing by "The Stone," did not resemble any kind of camaraderie I knew. These shouts came from the *moshav* members, all of whom would periodically gather in the club. This was called the "*moshav* assembly" and it had supreme authority, even more than the central committee.

By the entrance to the community hall was a large basalt rock that everyone called "The Stone." This was our hangout, just as in other places youngsters used to sit on metal sidewalk railings or around the neighborhood playground. It was there I had my first smoke and used my first swearword. On The Stone I eyed with envy older kids who had motor scooters and minitractors; after a wild ride they would stop there with a screech of the brakes to parade for the gaping admirers. On The Stone I sat with my best friends, who over the following two decades would distance themselves from me and from each other, each

---

* Meaning member, comrade, or friend.

15

off on his own orbit, and nothing would ever repair those friendships. But on The Stone we chatted and laughed and got bored together and looked for thrills. Some would break into the grocery shop and steal things, while others would sneak into the swimming pool on summer nights. Sometimes we would go out on "skirmishes" at the Home, a boarding school for needy children in the center of the village. We called them "the homers" and they called us "the villagers." In the battles held at recess in our joint school, the homers usually had the upper hand, because our gangs were no match for their sixth graders. But during evenings in the *moshav*, the tables turned. We had older brothers we could summon from The Stone.

To break the tedium, some of my friends would throw pomegranates that they picked from trees at the home of an elderly couple, the Frankels. Unfortunately for the Frankels, they lived very close to The Stone. We also exploded detonators and firecrackers, and set fire to potassium from the fertilizer storeroom to watch its blue flame. One time we burned magnesium from an illumination bomb, which we stole from one of our fathers' ammunition caches. It was unforgettable. For days afterward we all saw black and blue circles every time we closed our eyes, reminding us of the glare.

So everything revolved around The Stone. But on Holocaust Memorial Day—and to be exact, on *Yom Hazikaron* (a day commemorating Israel's fallen soldiers)—The Stone stood abandoned. Chinese lanterns, giving off a soft light, decorated both sides of the street from the parking lot to the community hall; these were really just brown paper bags half-filled with sand and a candle. They added a festive aura to the events of the day, and left The Stone bereft of its usual sitters. Although Holocaust Memorial Day was no time for pranks, some of my friends would "accidentally" brush the Chinese lanterns with their feet—not enough to overturn the lanterns, but enough to cause the paper bag to heat up so that in a matter of seconds, as the tripper walked away, it would completely burn out. But that really wasn't me, only perhaps some bad kid deep inside me. For on Holocaust Memorial Day, the general atmosphere simply wouldn't allow anything that wasn't all gravity and tears and awe. The adults didn't even yell when a kid was caught tampering with a lantern. They wouldn't scold, only mutter crossly through pursed lips: "You've performed sacrilege today, but because of the sanctity of the occasion I can't be properly cross with you."

CHAPTER 3

I acutely remember the unbearable feeling I experienced during one of those ceremonies. For years afterward it would flood back, filling me to bursting whenever I watched Holocaust Memorial Day films, black and white with horrible camera work. They showed naked, emaciated human beings piled on top of each other or stuffed into train cars, or standing in endless lines waiting to be incinerated, shot dead or just plain humiliated. It was in those Holocaust films that I was first exposed to the phenomenon of rape, for they often showed Nazi officers fattening up some scrawny Jewesses in order to turn them into soft, pleasant women. And I couldn't figure out how the hatred that led to such horrendous abuse and slaughter could exist alongside the love for which the women would be fed and groomed. Sex and the male sex drive were still unfamiliar to me then, so I resolved the contradiction by embracing the explanation I received from my parents and other authority figures: that the perpetrators were Nazis, were *absolute evil*, and such evil did not *make sense* the way normal people's actions did—and if there was no sense, naturally everything was possible.

But that unbearable feeling which I vividly recall from one of those ceremonies—which, perhaps, commemorated the Fallen Soldiers rather than the Holocaust—was as much about me as it was about the gruesome images in those films. It was the tormenting insight that I belong to this one miserable people. *Why me?* The question gnawed. *Why was I born to this fucked-up people?* A nation killed and slaughtered and raped as "the whole world kept silent," as Amiel, our legendary principal with his accordion and moustache and deep sonorous voice, would say at every ceremony in elementary school—and I would always wait patiently for these words, so overpowering, so frightening.

Why do I not belong to another people, any people? Why? I did not yet know, back then, that one could be born an Indian child in a village where drinking water is contaminated by human and cattle waste and the chances of reaching age five are slim. And I certainly couldn't imagine my mother trying to cure me, her baby, of diarrhea by depriving me of water to dry up the illness, as many Asian women do; in their attempt to stop the watery flow of feces, these women sometimes accidentally dehydrate their children to death. When I wondered why I couldn't be born to another people, I imagined a perfectly normal place—just like my village, only its inhabitants were not hated or persecuted or killed or incinerated, as in the films shown on Holocaust Memorial Day, or killed in Arab villages on a convoy to Gush Etzyon, lost and helpless.

The tale of the Gush Etzyon convoy belongs to that other Memorial Day, naturally, not to the Holocaust one. But for me they both possess one sense-memory. Not far from my home, some seventy years ago, lived Tuvya Kushnir. He grew up and went to school there, one of my uncontested childhood heroes. Tuvya loved plants (like me) and was "a loyal son to his people, his country, his homeland and village," as in the lofty lines inscribed on the Bible I received for my Bar Mitzvah from the congregation of the synagogue at my *moshav*. I too wanted to be a "loyal son to his people."

Tuvya grew up and became a soldier (like me), and because the Arabs held Jerusalem under siege—literally enclosed it all around with a high fence, a real wall, as they did to the Etzyon bloc as well, so I imagined—those poor people inside had no food or medication or ammunition to defend themselves. Tuvya, my childhood hero, and another thirty-four friends took off on foot carrying food and medication on their shoulders. They couldn't travel by car because the Arabs who were laying siege to Jerusalem had blocked the roads. That's why Rabin* and all the others were needed to break through those roads with armored trucks, but that is already another story. As a child, Tuvya would carry two pails of milk hanging from a yoke balanced on his shoulders. When the British soldiers saw him walking like that from the cowshed to the dairy, they probably thought the way I do now about the Indian farmers whom I see passing me by through my train car window. He worked hard as a young boy (like me), and that's why he was strong and sun-tanned and

---

* One of the siege-breakers in 1948. Almost half a century later, while serving as prime minister, he would be assassinated for seeking a peace treaty with the Palestinians.

handsome and ready to carry out the mission to provide food and medication to the poor people under siege. On the way they ran into an Arab shepherd. Since Tuvya and his friends were kind people (they were, after all, sons and brothers of survivors of the Holocaust in Europe, and they didn't carry on like barbarians), they let the shepherd go, only asking him to please not tell his Arab friends that they were going to Gush Etzyon on a secret mission to bring food and medication and ammunition, just for self-defense, for you know, Mr. Shepherd, what barbaric things your Arab brothers, who are not survivors nor sons of survivors, sometimes do. The shepherd turned out to be a bastard and told his buddies. They killed Tuvya and his friends and probably looted the food and medication—they sure turned out to be barbarians. If they had only learned from Esther, my Bible teacher, that "on the spoil laid they not their hand" . . . But good luck finding battlefield morals and Bible lore with those savages! Our guys were real heroes, they were few against many, pure against Arab, they fought to the last bullet and died together, loyal, strong, sun-tanned, handsome, pure (like me), and dead— so far not like me—although I yearned with all my heart to grow up and be like them, a loyal son to my people, country, homeland and village. Every year on Memorial Day I would stand and wait to hear Tuvya's name read among the Fallen of the *moshav*, and then I would shed a bereaved brother's tear. We would stand there with everyone else, not with the bereaved families, who were especially honored and had special tears and no one would get cross with their kids even if one of them did "accidentally" trip on a Chinese lantern.

CHAPTER 4

In fifth grade I took up the trumpet. In school we were informed of a special fund to help schools in the periphery—that is, in the weaker parts of the country—and that includes us too, not because we're weak but because we're far from the center and that's why we're entitled. Representatives of this fund came to test our diligence and sense of rhythm by asking us some questions and having us drum on a table. At the end of the test they informed me that I would play the trumpet. I remember this test as something very serious, and yet, when I talked about it at our Sabbath family dinner, my older cousin laughed at me. With one hand he rubbed circles on his belly and with the other, patted his head. When I couldn't imitate him, he said: "These are at least the skills of a trombone player." Then he stretched his right hand forward and his left hand back and announced: "Saxophone player." I joined the general mirth, although it dampened my enthusiasm over the prospect of becoming a trumpet player.

Nonetheless, playing the trumpet started me on a path that would eventually earn me prominence at official ceremonies, which in turn inflated the importance of ceremonies in my mind. There were ceremonies aplenty in our environment—memorial days commemorating the Holocaust, the fallen soldiers, improvised commemorations of Rabin at the public square or at school as one of the "candle kids."* There were recruiting festivities where the IDF marching song was played in honor of the graduating class leaving the *moshav* on their way to fulfill their national destiny. Music has the tremendous capacity to amplify feeling, and even when you're a musician of paltry talent like I was, it's thrilling to play a part in stirring up the audience.

I distinctly remember the first memorial ceremony where I played the trumpet. It was a total fiasco. IDF Memorial Day is a serious event where not even a snicker is tolerated. So no tomatoes were hurled at me on such a solemn occasion, but still some people bothered to comment: "Something went wrong there when you played." Or, "Don't worry, it happened to Ya'ara too when she was just a beginner." And, indeed, that ceremony signaled the passing of the baton from Ya'ara, the *moshav*'s ceremonial player—who was well on her way to the army band by then, to play at much larger and more important ceremonies in front of the Knesset or at the President's residence—to her successor, none other than myself. A few days prior to the ceremony, Ya'ara invited me to her home to choose

---

* Teenagers who lit candles as a mourning ritual following Rabin's assassination. They were also mourning the passing of the peace process.

23

the songs and practice. When Ya'ara's name would come up on the playground, kids would mockingly twist their right hand; her right hand was congenitally deformed and she even held the trumpet strangely. But I, six years her junior, was thrilled by her kindness to me and the seriousness with which she undertook the task at hand, as mentor and friend.

We chose "Eli, Eli"* and "Hatikva,"† of course. Most importantly, we practiced the flag-lowering bugle call that would open the ceremony. Ya'ara made up a second part for herself and let me play the lead part so that at the ceremony she could not cover for me. Thus, although she played her second part impeccably, this "Eli, Eli" was outrageous. I squeaked quite a bit through the bugle call, too. At the close of one of our rehearsals, when the ceremony organizer suggested I practice a bit more, Ya'ara told me: "Look, we're being mocked." I realized it was only me being mocked. The organizer hinted that I was too small to rise up to the occasion, but Ya'ara really made things easier for me. After the ceremony I felt terrible and didn't fiddle with any Chinese lanterns. I just wanted my parents to stop chatting with their friends so I could get the hell out of there.

---

* Short poignant invocation of God hailing the simple beauty of creation and expressing one's yearning for it never to end, written by one of Israel's pre-State heroes, Hanna Senesh. Senesh was captured, tortured and killed by the Nazis after parachuting behind enemy lines in an attempt to save her Hungarian-Jewish community during the Holocaust.

† The national anthem.

CHAPTER 5

The truth is, my favorite moment in those ceremonies was the announcement that "the ceremony is over," uttered in a deep official voice, releasing the public from its self-conscious stance at attention for the anthem "Hatikva." Everyone knows when the singing's over, the last verse is even repeated — "To be a free nation in our homeland, land of Zion and Jeru-u-u-u-salem" — and then people remain standing for another strange moment, pleasant perhaps but a bit embarrassing, too, until one of the people with the black sheets of paper decorated by yellow Stars-of-David steps gravely up to one of the microphones, inhales deeply, stalls another tiny moment—his moment of power—and says "the ceremony is over."

My second favorite moment was "Yizkor"* — not the prayer itself but the title. One of the chaps with the black sheets of paper would step up to the microphone. He would wait for a silence that did not always come, for in the back rows people would not have noticed him yet, and some people would still

---

* The "remembrance" prayer.

be sitting down, and there would be a kid who had just burnt a Chinese lantern and some mother who crossly, quietly muttered at him, and some dog barking, and again someone would mutter through clenched teeth: "Why do those idiots not tie up their dog? Good God, it's Holocaust Memorial Day. Even today?" The fellow behind the microphone knew full well that the slightest clearing of his throat would hush the crowd instantly. But usually he does not clear his throat. He would simply say "Yizkor," strongly emphasizing the "kor," and then for three or four seconds a deathly silence would fall upon the gathering, even the jackals in the nearby ravine must have realized something important was taking place, and again that "Yizkor," this time accompanied by "The People of Israel" and so on and so forth. In between "Yizkor" and "The ceremony is over" all sorts of sad, touching texts were recited, snivels were held back, male eyes fogged over, tears flowed down women's cheeks. In between there were also musical intermezzos meant to move or please the audience.

My trumpet playing made me a vital participant in every single memorial ceremony. Before Ya'ara's time, however, the flag was lowered on Memorial Days to the sound of the saxophone or even the French horn, and before that, so the legend goes, it was simply lowered to the beat of a drum. Unlike the state flag at the Knesset, the flag at the village was lowered on Memorial Day but not raised again full mast on the morrow, Independence Day, because on Independence Day everyone climbed Mount Gilboa. People used to ascend en masse and play organized games such as tug-of-war, volleyball and dodge ball. There were team games of girls against boys, dairy versus chicken-coop workers, veteran *moshav* members against new ones. We were the new ones, though I never figured out how this was possible, since I was born there and was already grown up, but apparently a new member remains new for good, and in our parts special honor is due the founding fathers. Eventually, when the social adhesives melted in the heat of the region, and greening-the-wasteland was no longer a noble cause, the communal picnics died out as well. In the spirit of tradition and Independence Day festivities, many still climb up Mount Gilboa to make chicken and beef sacrifices but each family celebrates on its own. These memories of a united community climbing the slope, playing dodge ball and tug-of-war, marching in my mind along with my memory of being stuffed to bursting with grilled meat—I merely mention them here so you might understand how this came about, how we could forget to raise the flag back up on Independence Day. And so our flag always remained at half mast, and still every year we would lower it anew, as if to verify that we still do get very sad. For me this was rather convenient, as the bugle call for lowering the flag was much easier to play than the call for raising it.

The price for not having practiced the bugle call for raising the flag was paid in full years later, in Santiago de Chile, when I was called upon to play during both lowering and raising of the flag. I tried to fake it. The musical director of the ceremony, a respected pianist in the Jewish community, had perfect pitch, and my bad pitch confused her senses. The flag rose slowly, but

I didn't manage to rise in the scale all the way to the high note. It was slightly embarrassing but I didn't think about it too much, for that Independence Day I was wholly devoted to attempting to lift the skirt of Miriam, one of the Jewish school girls.

Counting Chile (where I spent a nice long time at my uncle's house), the Czech Republic and Poland (where I went on our high school Holocaust study tour), and Germany (where I went on a youth "friendship mission" from the Gilboa region), I lowered flags and trumpeted the strains of "Hatikvah" in five countries. This was quite a record for someone who did not proceed to enlist in the IDF band. Instead, I put on combat fatigues and become a fighter, moved as I was by the Holocaust Memorial Day and IDF Memorial Day ceremonies. In eleventh grade, when my music teacher told me he had prepared a series of lessons to get me ready for the IDF band auditions and promised that at my present level I would do very well, I sneered: "I want to be a combatant, a fighter. So these preparations are unnecessary." He tried to persuade me to change my mind. He said that if I chose not to join the band, I had no chance of becoming a musician in the future. "You are giving up everything you have invested in the seven years of your music studies," he said. "Good," I answered. "Let's get on with class." I enjoyed hearing him declare that this was a significant moment in my life, a moment of decision. It only made me more determined to go running three times a week, six kilometers at a time around the *moshav* fields, getting ready for the select unit preparatory training.

As an educational activity on Memorial Day, our high school principal invited some lieutenant colonel of the armor corps to speak to us. The lieutenant colonel was a native of nearby *moshav* Hayogev and an alumnus. The principal's voice dripped with pride as he introduced the guest, as if he himself had trained the lieutenant colonel to escape anti-tank missiles or had crawled with him up and down sand dunes in basic training. The officer showed us a clip in which a heavy tank stampeded the Negev Desert sands, spitting fire and blasting metal jalopies. At the end of the ride, the tank halted in a cloud of dust and a female soldier emerged from it, taking off her helmet and shaking out her long blonde hair like some shampoo advertisement. This was, as it were, an appeal to the girls, and it was accompanied by an explanation of how they could contribute to the cause as armor corps instructors. But it was also an appeal to us boys, with our hunger for power and sex. What sells better than a slim, tall blonde climbing out of a tank? And not just any tank, but the "world's best" tank in the "world's strongest army." What could be more attractive to an adolescent who could not hear his physics teacher for the sheer flood of nude women performing pornographic dance moves in his mind, filling the space between him and the blackboard?

The lieutenant colonel used allegory to explain our role in the coming years. He described a soldier as a stretcher bearer, nearly collapsing from fatigue but confident that in a few seconds his mate would step up to replace him. Our older friends, now tearing themselves to shreds for three years and bearing the burden of security, were waiting for us to step up as one man and replace them for our allotted time, before getting on with our own lives. I used this romantic allegory myself a few years later to try and motivate my own subordinates. And bidding farewell to my commanders and subordinates, I even made a poem of it, in thanks, for posterity in our company book.

In one of the Holocaust Memorial Day documentary films, someone said that after what had happened in Europe "an armed Jew is sexy." I don't recall whose words these were, but they etched themselves in my memory and accompanied me all through my military service. When I was ousted from the pilot-training course, I had some choices to make again. Every "flying cadet" dropped from the course at a late stage is offered a convenient, lucrative home-front assignment. It was easy to relinquish the elitist air force for the sake of becoming an armed Jew. After all, I wanted to be sexy.

CHAPTER 6

I began to train for my encounter with you, the girl who stole my Holocaust, when I was ten years old, about your age. Much later my main practice took place in basic and advanced combat training, where I learned to dash from one dugout to another, crawl, aim my gun barrel with a sharp eye and carefully squeeze the trigger, believing in my power and willing to make the greatest of sacrifices. But this was only the final stage of the body and mind training that had started in my early childhood.

In officers' school too, I was trained for our encounter. This time I learned to make those soldiers you saw following me, run, crawl, and shoot when I ordered them to do so, and always keep their gaze sharply focused for their guns to follow.

There are practice routines that precede certain missions. "Standard operating procedures," they're called. Before arresting a wanted man, we would practice the procedure. Before demolishing a house, the men would practice. And lying in ambush was preceded by a tedious and complex briefing. You had to learn how to disappear into the ground so that even if a child rode by on a donkey extremely close to us, he wouldn't notice us, and if his kid brother came running after him, he wouldn't spot the change in the topography of his own yard until he literally fell into our superbly camouflaged hiding place. He would then be shackled, blindfolded and perhaps even gently smacked. He would be told that he was out of his mind—he could not possibly have seen what he just saw.

From that moment on he remembered nothing. Total darkness took over and a horrible silence fell all around. He wanted to scream but couldn't, he wanted to beg forgiveness but knew not of whom. He understood nothing and anyway, no one would believe a word he said. Maybe he better keep it to himself. Do you understand this, little girl?

Prior to such a mission, standard operating procedures were necessary because it was no simple matter to plant a camera facing the window of that grandfather, in whose yard the dark forces of evil assembled. The only possible hideout on that barren rocky hill was underground. We had to reach the exact spot, disguised in advance as that rocky landscape. We had to get rid of our scent. We had to piss, shit and eat in the crowded hideout without leaving a trace. We had to be replaced every twenty-four hours by a new group of soldiers without being discovered. And naturally, we had to prepare for the worst. And the worst, little girl, was a nine-year-old kid running through his grandfather's yard and falling right into our laps.

The mission in which my Holocaust was stolen was not at all planned, so obviously we had not trained for it. There were no standard operating procedures, not even a concise daily briefing; there was no navigation track to be studied, no gear parade, no briefing on rules of engagement nor possible scenarios of eventualities and responses. However, I had already begun to prepare for it when I was still a child.

In third grade we played a game of "illegal immigrants" against "the Brits." My father played a principal role in the game: he brought along an authentic Sten gun from Mr. Shem Tov's weapon collection, preserved in the *moshav* ever since his *Palmah** days. He even brought along a strange balaclava made of greenish-brown wool that had two points jutting out of the sides.

In our game, we pretended to be Jewish underground Hagannah fighters battling the British colonial police. We marched through the darkness towards the beach, where other kids were waiting. These kids played the role of new illegal immigrants to the land that would become Israel. They disembarked, as it were, from their rickety boats. Their faces were the picture of despair. They carried the square suitcases of yesteryear and they all repeated the Hebrew phrase that the Hagannah supreme command had taught them: "I am a Jew in Eretz Israel," "I am a Jew in Eretz Israel." We "Hagannah heroes" repeated the same phrase in order to blend in with the immigrants. And so the Brits, the bad guys in this game, couldn't tell who was a sun-tanned Hebrew-speaking Sabra fighter and who was a new immigrant. These immigrants, coming from faraway places,

---

* Pre-State commando troops.

knew not a word of Hebrew, the language without which the Jews would never be a nation, as was written over our school-house doorway: "Two things without which Jews will never be a nation: the land and the language."

This was how the Jewish underground fooled the Brits and smuggled in the illegal immigrants who went on to fight the Arabs and made room for us in this country, which was nearly empty anyway to begin with. If the Arabs had not started the fighting, we never would have even needed the war, for we have always sought only peace. Then the illegal immigrants learned the language and this is how we became a nation.

But that was only a childish game. By the time I was ten years old, Jews were allowed to come here and there was no more need to smuggle in illegal immigrants.

Not knowing I would eventually run into you, my little thief, my first real soldiering was as early as the fourth grade — our initiation into night maneuvers in our youth movement. We went out for *hag ha'ma'alot*, the holiday on which a ceremony of fire inscriptions and torches marks the start of a new year. Every age group would rise up the movement ranks towards the superior levels of counseling and fulfillment, from childhood to youth and on to soldiering in full faith.

Before our first night maneuvers, our excitement knew no bounds. I remember trying on a khaki army belt at home. My mother fit it with a canteen, camouflaged in olive green like the rest of my kit and filled with water. I wore the belt with the canteen over my dark blue shirt, dark enough for night and thick enough to protect me from the thorns we would crawl over while training—"Fall! Crawl! Aim! Range! Fire!" The color blue also stood for simple labor, for we were farmers' children after all. The shirt was embellished with a red ribbon, for we were socialists as well and believed in the right of every man to equality and liberty. The shirt was tucked into thick blue work trousers that had to be rolled up because they were real adults' work clothes, and I was short even for my own age.

Evening approached and preparations peaked. For weeks we had slaved over the fire inscription of our group's name: "*Lahav.*"* We wrapped sacking around metal wire and dipped it in diesel fuel. Each group prepared an inscription bearing its name, along with another inscription such as "*Laavoda, Lahagana Velashalom*": ("For work, for defense, for peace!"), which was the movement's motto. The inscriptions would be put up at the basalt quarry out in the *moshav* fields by the older counselors and ninth-graders.

On the night of the holiday the different groups marched to the fire ceremony one by one. The younger kids were told to expect a surprise at the end, and there were rumors galore about what the surprise would be.

We marched uphill on a dirt track. Dark had fallen all around and we walked further and further from the *moshav* lights, our familiar sense of security fading slowly, replaced by a certain pleasant fear, the kind we knew from galloping on a horse through the *moshav* fields. We passed by the last goat shed and the old water tower.

---

* "Blade," but also "flame."

"Hey, we're on our way to the cemetery," someone whispered, mainly to break the silence and perhaps even to relieve our fear.

"Shhh . . . quiet!" the counselor scolded us.

"This Yaron can't take anything seriously," Jonathan whispered to Michal, as she walked next to him in the line.

Secretly, I envied Jonathan for getting ahead of me, again, with his mature, brave talk. Yaron fell silent. He understood very well, as did the other fourteen kids in the group, that we were doing something serious. The lines marched deeper into the dark. On our left was a citrus grove with its threatening shadows, on our right was a vast field of grain. None of us knew where we were headed. We just repeated to ourselves in silence the orders we had received in our last training session.

At this last training session, our counselor was Kfir, who was not very popular. He was pale and pimply and not the kind of counselor-idol that Elad or Omri were; Elad or Omri were real men who went on to become naval commandos. When Kfir gave us our night maneuver instructions, he said that when we heard someone shout "grenade!" we were to stand still. But his two co-counselors, Hadar and Ella, felt he was making a horrible mistake. The three began to whisper to each other, but then a loud voice shouted, "No arguing in front of the kids!"

We enjoyed the authority crisis taking place in front of our very eyes. Two of the counselors went out to inquire with the elder counselor, who knew about real army stuff. When they came back, Kfir corrected himself. He said that when we hear "grenade!" we should obviously jump sideways and count:

Twenty-one, twenty-two, twenty-three, and, boom! Whoever did not lie down in the ditch by the road, curled up with his hands over his head, was already dead for sure. And Kfir added that he knew this, of course, but earlier he had been talking about a lighting grenade—so when we hear someone yell "projector!" we really should stay put like statues, because the British sentries light up the area from their towers and look for movement.

On the real night maneuvers, when we heard "grenade!" we jumped into the thorny bushes. And we stood as still as statues when we heard "projector!" While walking, we kept the proper spacing between us—not so far that we couldn't maintain eye contact, but not so close as to get blasted by the same explosive charge. When the counselor whispered "count off!" to the kid at the front of the line, that kid quietly passed it on to the next kid, and so on until the count reached the counselor at the back of the line. Then that counselor would whisper "one" to the kid at the back of the line, and the count would eventually reach the front of the line again. Everything was done while walking, and it all had to take place as quietly as humanly possible.

With the years, these counts became simple. Unlike the treks in the army where the guy in front of me would be sweaty and tired. On that first night march I followed a pretty girl and was eager for the next count so I could move two steps ahead, place a secure hand on her shoulder and say "six," while inhaling some of her body scent. After all, in full daylight I would never dare place a hand on that shoulder: she would see me blush and I wouldn't know what to whisper to her. And here came night maneuvers to my rescue, making sure that I didn't get lost in the fields or lynched by an Arab gang or kidnapped by the Brits, and allowing me—ordering me, in fact—to whisper into a pretty girl's ear over and over again.

After the long trek, we stopped and gathered in silence. We were told that we were to be accepted into the secret fold of the movement, and that the acceptance ceremony would take place on top of a nearby hill. And since the hill was infested with enemies, we would have to sneak up in pairs. Two by two we ventured forth up the hill. On the way we encountered a British sentry with a torch. When the torchlight got close to us we froze as we had practiced, and in the last meters near the top we crawled among the basalt rocks and summer thorns.

At the top sat the secret commanders with masked faces. They read aloud an oath and made us sign it with our thumbs dipped in blood-like gouache paint. We swore to remain loyal and keep the secret and fulfill any mission we were assigned in love and good faith. One by one we swore and then marched together to the fire ceremony. A burning ball descended from the cliff and lit a huge torch, which was passed from group to group. There were greetings and songs, and then came the great surprise, which everyone except for us neophytes knew about already: our parents came there in cars, stayed with us for the ceremony and—special treat— drove us home afterwards.

At one of the youth summer camps I attended—I no longer recall whether it was "In the Footsteps of Warriors Camp," or

"Commando-Underground-Fighters-Against-the-Brits Camp" or perhaps even "Camp of the People of Israel"—I had a special role in night maneuvers. I walked at the end of the line with my friend Ran, who was much cooler and better-looking than I. When the call "grenade!" rang out, we lay down last, facing each other. After waiting on the ground for a long time, we had to make sure none of the kids had fallen asleep—from battle fatigue, or from staying up late to pull pranks, like painting the faces of the girls while they slept or stealing flags from nearby encampments. Ran and I knew we were putting ourselves at risk, but we also knew it was for the good of the whole force. Just like Nathan Elbaz did.

Nathan Elbaz was a soldier who sacrificed his own life to save his fellow soldiers. He was not an admired fighter—his job was to neutralize the detonators of grenades in the bunker tent. One day in the bunker tent, he suddenly heard the worst click of them all—the detonator on a grenade he was holding had somehow been activated. Nathan had four vital seconds to decide what to do. He ran out of the bunker to a nearby ditch, but saw many fellow soldiers there, so he turned back and again saw his beloved friends: Whose life would he sacrifice? He chose himself. He held the grenade close to his chest and jumped on it and died for the sake of everyone in the camp.

This story was often told in the youth movement around Memorial Day or right before a night maneuver. With his death Nathan Elbaz taught us the meaning of comradeship, sacrifice, life. With his death he taught us how to live. I wanted to cry for him but I couldn't afford to be a crybaby in front of the whole group. On one Memorial Day, our counselor asked us if we would do what Nathan Elbaz the hero did: after all, he could have thrown the grenade far away and then his mates would only have been wounded, and he wouldn't have been hurt at all. But no, not Nathan Elbaz. He didn't risk his friends' lives. He jumped on the grenade.

At that time there were still battle and sacrifice stories mixed up in my mind with tales of vampires threatening to suck my blood. But Nathan Elbaz really did jump over the grenade. His story was real. Unlike the vampire stories, there was no surprise ending that saved everyone from danger. Instead, at the end of Nathan's story was the question: Would you do as he did? Would you die for our sake? And you?

And you, wouldn't you want heroic tales to be told about you? Imagine that every year a group of children sat by the spring with their counselor, a counselor in sandals, a blue shirt and shorts, who would tell them fascinating, thrilling stories in which you were the heroine. I did. I wanted stories to be told about me, about my courage, my resourcefulness and cleverness. I dreamt of being a battle hero.

In the meantime, we continued jumping into thorn bushes on night maneuvers and crawling to the flag at summer camp. Years later, this know-how would help me get to you safely.

CHAPTER 7

Like everyone else, I traveled to Poland with our school delegation. We Jewish Israeli high school students got to visit the death-camp of Auschwitz and other Holocaust commemoration sites as a part of our national grooming, a year before we graduated and enlisted in the military. On the same bus as our group was a delegation from the Israel Air Force technical school, so we had boys in uniform. Throughout the trip, the Air Force flag was flown along with the Israeli flag, all the more impressive and official looking for it.

In Poland, too, I was writing. I wrote because that is what you're supposed to do—it was healthy and liberating, or so we were told—and also because I wanted to be one of those people who, at Holocaust Memorial Day ceremonies, read out what he himself had written instead of some banal, well-known poem or psalm. And indeed, when we returned I did read one of my writings aloud at both the school and the *moshav* ceremonies:

I am walking inside the museum at Auschwitz and looking at the piles of shoes. I choose a shoe and try to imagine its

41

owner. Here's a pink little crybaby girl's shoe, there's a dark shoe of a respectable gentleman and pillar of the community. I try to dress those people in the rest of their clothing, and then proceed to give them their shape and gait and a face and eyes and a gaze. I try to hear them talking, but my attempt to imagine an unfamiliar language fails. Here is a pair of large boots, surely of a fifty-year-old man, perhaps even sixty, white-haired, his cheeks plump and his smile broad. A fairly large paunch peeps under an old faded blue cloth jacket, his rough dark trousers held up with a worn leather belt, the pant legs too short so that the heavy boots lying there in front of me show underneath. And that grandfather left his home in town yesterday and was taken here. His home was probably not much different from the houses we saw through the windows of our bus on the way here, a little wooden house surrounded by a garden, summer flowers blooming between the vegetable beds. In winter smoke billowed out of the chimney and a fire heated the small space where his family slept. His children had already left home. One of them went to study at the yeshivah and became a scholar, but the three others learnt a trade and moved to the city, got married and raised children. They have new ideas and don't ever attend the synagogue. He himself still lives with his wife in the same wooden hut where he was born. Every night as he comes home from the market, where he is employed as a coachman, he stops at the nearby woods to chop some wood for heating. When he gets home, his wife is still working in the garden and the chickens scurry around her, pecking. He unloads the wood off his aching back and they go inside together and have supper—dark bread, cooked barley grits, a chunk of hard cheese and hot tea. This simple, hard, pleasant life came to a sudden halt when this grandfather, who for a few moments is mine as well, was arrested, stuffed into a cattle car and brought here. His heavy boots were taken off, he was stripped, showered, shaved, suffocated, incinerated. His smoke scattered in this sky right here, his ashes thrown into the clear water of the river flowing nearby. This is how I went on and scanned many pairs of shoes, and created people, and invented their lives.

In Poland I was proud and happy. The piles of shoes and ash at Auschwitz and Maidanek, and the stories of the witness who accompanied us (who had been one of Dr. Mengele's "children"), the descriptions of starvation in the woods—all these are not exactly a recipe for happiness, of course, but still I was happy.

At Auschwitz I wept as I read the names of all the Labendiks who had been killed. Labendik was the name of my paternal grandfather before he changed it to the Hebrew name Chayut (vitality)—a rather absurd name to bear in the death camps. I wept at the hall with its commemorative candles and sang the *kaddish*, the traditional Jewish prayer for the dead, in a deep sad voice with a list of names in my hand. I burst into very real tears and wept for a very long time, a loud, visceral, unstoppable weeping. It was the first time I ever read this list that we were asked to bring along and my mother had prepared for me before we left. It was photocopied from the town register of Sokolka. What a horrible list: names and names and more names, truly depressing.

I had not worked on a roots project in the seventh grade, not even copied my sisters' projects, as did many other third sons of deep-rooted families. I was lazy, just as I was too lazy to photocopy that list myself or at least give it a glance before our departure, and that's why I didn't know how large my family had been. And perhaps, too, because my grandfather passed away long before I was born and my grandmother did not even live long enough to celebrate my father's Bar Mitzvah, and so I had no one to relate that huge murdered family to. But that shocking list removed all the brakes and opened my floodgates. Only now did I realize that out of so many, only my father and one aunt—his sister—were left, and that we seven cousins would have numbered dozens or even hundreds of people.

The anger, the sorrow, the shame and the unwillingness to be a part of all this—the emotions I felt towards my Holocaust when I was a young child—were now replaced by entirely different emotions. Now, in Poland, as a high school adolescent, I began to sense belonging, self-love, power and pride, and the desire to contribute, to live and be strong, so strong that no one would ever try to hurt me.

I remember the tones of "Hatikvah" as I played my trumpet in the death camps of Poland, and a year earlier in the German concentration camp at Buchenwald, which I visited with a

German-Israeli friendship delegation of youth—the strongest sensation I had had back then was the desire to take revenge.

As I played I took revenge on all those who hated us. If any Nazi villain, I thought, is hiding in Argentina or Brazil, if some miserable train worker of that war is now sitting in his living room in Germany or Poland, he is surely going crazy at the thought that in spite of all the extermination efforts, our State has come into being. A whole nation was gathered from all corners of the earth to the land of its forefathers to found a mighty army and build national waterways and highways, and glass skyscrapers in Tel Aviv. And that nation sent me to the country of this Nazi villain to play our national anthem, full of hope—*tikvah*.

Wherever they might be, those scum-of-the-earth criminals, they were now tormented by my vengeful playing, our vengeance in being proud Jewish boys, a vengeance mightier than any court sentence, more painful, even, than the hangman's noose. That melody echoed in the ears of our haters and proved that in spite of the registers of the victims that we read, weeping, and despite the ashes of all those who were incinerated, and the piles of shoes and spectacles and gold teeth pulled out and shipped directly to Switzerland, in spite of it all, we were strong. And I was here and I was blowing the trumpet D-E-F-G-A-A for "Hatikvah" and B-B-F#-G for "My God, my God, may it never be over / The sand and the sea, the rustling water / The glittering sky, man's prayer."*

---

* "Eli, Eli."

This was sweet revenge. I drew power from my Holocaust and this power pushed me on, to want to enlist and serve in a select recon unit, possibly in the Nahal, for my dad served there and that would strengthen my roots. (And also because there are fewer bullies in the Nahal and my time there would be more fun.) But this is only in parentheses because frankly I am all for integration, and a melting pot the likes of our army exists nowhere else in the world.

This was the force that later pushed me to go to officers' training at the end of my training as a combatant. Other options of assignment made by my commanders were tempting and even flattering and much in demand, and I wasn't exactly one of my team's favorites, to put it mildly. And rightly so.

I was one of those who told on the commander who cheated on exams and who opened a map during navigation maneuvers. I had been instructed that "credibility and truth are foremost in the army," but I never realized they didn't really mean it. Even years later, when I would join Breaking the Silence and would tell anyone, any journalist who listened, how houses were blasted and what it was like to use a human shield and how it felt to command a dozen soldiers and 2,500 Palestinians on a normal "workday" at Qalandiya Checkpoint—even then I would still think that credibility and truth come first.

It would take a long time for me to gradually realize that for many people, truth is worth nothing. When I realized this I was deeply disappointed in human nature, just as I felt when, as a child, I discovered what rape was and was ashamed of being male, and just as I felt when I discovered how many guys cheated on pilot training exams. There were only a few nerds who watched their ass and they didn't really mind what the others did. When the squadron commander arrived to deliver a speech about credibility and warned us not to cheat, I wondered whether he had once been one of the few nerds and not like all the rest. Suddenly, I didn't believe him. I got sick to my stomach and cried that night, cried like a kid on the shoulder of my buddy, the other nerd in the course.

I cried because I missed my girlfriend, and because of the lies. Everyone lied. Even I lied. I had lied to her two years earlier. I had gone as a "young ambassador" to represent our country in Argentina and Chile. I told them what a cool place Israel was and that they shouldn't listen to the news about us because everyone lied and we in Israel only wanted peace, and that boys and children were the same everywhere, maybe except for those in countries where they are brainwashed and it was not their fault. There, in Chile, I kissed the daughter of the man in charge of education in the region. We even made out in the back seat of the car, when her father drove us to our next destination. And now I was crying because I hadn't confessed this to my beloved, my girlfriend who was not waiting for me at home like she did two years ago, loving and loyal, and I was a wretched liar like everyone else. What a crisis that was. The irony is that the friend on whose shoulders I cried would wait not even twenty-four hours after I broke up with that love of my youth before he took her under his wing and invited her to cry on his shoulder—not just any shoulder. It was the shoulder of a pilot, a tall and handsome pilot.

I was sent on this mission to Chile and Argentina on behalf of the Ministry of Foreign Affairs when I was in the eleventh grade. We traveled in couples as "young ambassadors" and stayed overnight with host families, mainly from the Jewish communities but also with families of non-Jewish Zionist supporters. We spoke at schools, universities, youth movements and even at one Christian church. We projected an official silent PR film and spoke of our country's beauty, sanctity and uniqueness. We said that in our country new drivers tagged their car with a yellow sign so everyone would know they couldn't drive very well yet, and this always made our audience laugh. We would show the audience this "new driver" sign and use it to demonstrate the special Hebrew alphabet, which we said was written from right to left. We wrote our names on the board and even the names of a few people in the audience.

The most amusing part for us was to explain our country's miniature proportions, as we fitted its whole length into the width of narrow Chile. Or all of it into the tiny province of Tucuman in Argentina—they simply couldn't believe it. We amazed them by telling them the obvious: that as Deborah, my fellow traveler, explained, "Soon we will enlist, he for three years, I for two," and added how important it was for us to contribute to our country, and how normal and obvious it was for us that the army was the next phase in our lives, after school and before the "big trip" and college.

At every lecture we gave, Deborah and I raised the topic of the Holocaust and its inevitable lesson: that our country, the

State of Israel, must exist and be strong. The idea of talking about the Holocaust was mine, but Deborah played the principal role in this show. At times she made the audience weep as she told about her survivor grandmother who could not possibly throw away food, not even a single crumb, and forced the whole family to eat everything on their plates, down to the last morsel. And if there were still leftovers, she collected them and ate them herself or saved them for the next meal. Before one of the lectures I suggested she let up a bit, and in this spirit I even changed our usual commentary during the film. She was very cross at me and for nearly two days we hardly spoke to each other.

Slowly, the telling of the Holocaust became our mission's main topic. I recall how one evening, in the province of Misiones, Argentina, I touched the heart of the mother of our host family. We spoke about the Holocaust and the refugees who arrived on a rickety boat from blood-drenched Europe and immediately went forth to fight the Arabs. I described in detail the myth of the Jew who migrated to Palestine on his own, without any family relations, disembarked in Jaffa port, was handed a gun and ran east to fight for Jerusalem and fell there on one of its rocky hills, and now he is buried nameless, and has no one to mourn him or honor his memory. That is why we as a nation must mourn and honor this refugee, whose force and valiance all of the seven Arab states together could not defeat. I spoke about the successors of this refugee in Israel's subsequent wars, and when I got to 1967 — the conquest of the Wailing Wall, the unification of Jerusalem and the nation's broken heart—her tears flowed. Tears that must have already sprung earlier when she thought of her father, how he sailed alone to Argentina at the end of that war, and but for his luck, he too might have reached Jaffa and run on from there to some Jerusalem hill, and then she would not have been born, nor would her large house exist, neither her great wealth nor her daughter, about my age, who sat at the table throughout this conversation, completely bored.

And so my brain—washed with a single dogmatic truth— combined with my youthful innocence and my skill at moving hearts made tears flow in faraway Argentina. I kept those tears in my memory along with the tears I gathered while reading aloud what I had written about the imaginary grandfather in Poland. The next tears I proceeded to reap were tears of the love for homeland and flag, tears proud and uplifted, tears of rich Jews and very rich American Jewish mothers and grand- mothers, tears falling on checks and contracts for investments in bonds, which we collected every evening.

But that chapter of my story will have to wait. First, as I promised, I'll tell you about the girl who stole my Holocaust.

CHAPTER 8

I don't know the name of the thief, but her image is deeply etched in my memory. Her complexion is lighter than that of her fellow villagers. Her eyes are black and large, set off by long dusty eyelashes. Her height is that of a ten-year-old and she is thin, very thin. Her shoulder blades protrude.

On the day of the theft, she wore a light-colored garment that I can't exactly describe, but I remember how, at the moment of the deed itself, when she finally looked away and began to run with her back to me, it fluttered against her bony body. The air was still on that hot, hazy day on the northern slopes of the Jerusalem hills. And yet that light-colored garment billows in my memory. Seeing her run was a familiar sight and seemed almost natural, so I realized very late that this child had run off with the most precious emotional and spiritual possession I had inherited from my forefathers — my Holocaust.

I didn't know your village, my little thief. It was not one of those "wasps' nests" — that is how we referred to the "hostile" or "trouble-spot" villages that we frequented in order to "make a show of presence." This meant rumbling through them, raising a racket, hurling teargas canisters into markets and balconies, blasting stun grenades, amusedly yelling swearwords over the commander's Jeep loudspeaker, firing live ammunition at house walls, piles of dirt and trash or vineyard terraces. I knew such villages like the palm of my hand.

I knew where stones would be thrown and where I could walk about safely, smiling, without wearing a helmet. I knew where a Jeep could be parked without being noticed and where passers-by could be taken by surprise at our show of force. I knew where we mustn't enter because exiting that alley would take too long and the stone- and stick-hurlers would have plenty of time to jeer as we remained caged in our Jeep.

"I am no sucker," the first Israeli I met in India, at the New Delhi airport, told me. "I let myself be screwed once in every country and then, then I learn my lesson and it never happens again, no way!" He was on his way to see his regular yoga teacher to calm down a bit. And he really needed to calm down, who doesn't? That's how it was in the Occupied Territories, too: I was no sucker and if I got screwed once with a hail of stones, sticks and curses, fine. Once, I entered that street, and it was a mistake that someone had to pay for; someone always pays for those first, one-time mistakes. For example, a kid paid for running slowly while trying to escape chaos. He was caught and shackled in front of his mother or older sister, who screamed and wept, and he was thrown into the Jeep, driven an hour's walk away, then lightly pushed out of the Jeep. I don't remember whether we freed his hands or let the other price-payers do it. Anyway, we figured, this kid learned his lesson.

And it was not only kids who were there to pay for the humiliation we felt after making such mistakes. Shopkeepers, too, paid when we fired teargas into their shops because we thought the curses or stones had originated there. Or their name was very similar to one of the names on our wanted list. Or their shop was on Shaheed Street, and Shaheed, we all thought, means terrorist, so it makes sense that on "terrorist" street we'll find the guilty parties who must pay for humiliating us.

This was all done in order to "make them pay the price for disturbing the peace"—these were the exact words used in written orders when the authorities wanted to define the need for scapegoats. These orders needed to be confirmed by the upper echelons, but that did not mean that we always had to use gas canisters to make our point clear. We could just park the armed personnel carrier or Jeep in front of the shop and eat our warm meal there, brought along specially for this mission. Hear some music, have a good meal, if the right cook was on the right shift. And also "show presence." The shopkeeper would beg us to go enjoy ourselves elsewhere, because otherwise no customers would come in, and he hadn't earned anything anyway since that whole shit began. Interesting, what he meant by "since the whole shit began." We had been in that area only two or three months and it smelled as though the shit has always been there . . . "You should have thought of this before you let them hurl stones from the roof of the apartment above your shop," someone would tell him, while chewing some mashed potatoes or a meat patty. While the shopkeeper begged, flattered the soldiers, and cursed Arafat and the rest of the PA leaders, he also carried out our mission impeccably. He shooed away any boy or child and yelled at the youngsters running on the rooftops and sometimes even caught someone who may have been there yesterday and beat him to a pulp, beat him up as we never would. After all, we are no Arabs.

Her village was not like that. So in spite of its proximity to our camp, I wasn't familiar with the place. The village vineyards bordered on the camp and we only had to drive ten minutes to enter: exit the camp to the main road and cross the barbed wire "barrier." "Barrier"—the official appellation of the Separation Fence when it was first erected. Sometimes the barrier consisted of a mere pile of barbed wire coils—"curlies"—which were sometimes used for stage sets in Holocaust Memorial ceremonies. At other times the barrier might consist of a pothole, or a ditch dug in the rock, or a dirt pile. Our mission that day was as simple as could be: "escorting" civil administration officials.

Such escorts were usually easy and uneventful. But they sometimes included interesting encounters with "special forces," such as police officers sent to search for stolen Jewish property in Palestinian towns; or *Shabak* General Security Services agents who spoke very little and always wore tense, impressive faces, their weapons—incidental as they were— shining under their dark jackets. We also escorted Engineering Corps units who sampled the bedrock, and waterworks employees who searched for water or planned pipeline routes, or employees of cellular phone companies and private contractors sent to put up antennas or connect residential trailers of Israeli settlers to the power grid.

We also escorted senior army officers who for some reason never followed the orders they themselves had issued and wouldn't let us check the area before they rode through in their less-armored cars, so that our escort really had nothing to do with their security. They looked on with contempt, always, and we were especially amused to see how our tough, cruel deputy battalion commander would scurry around them like a chicken and explain and apologize in an unfamiliarly patient tone and note down their scolds and reprimands in his book as though these were direct orders to be promptly carried out.

Thus our commander faced the general, as I faced him and on down the chain of command, down to the child who was too slow to run away and would pay for the humiliation suffered by the legendary deputy battalion commander as the general scolded him in front of his subordinates.

Anyway, the escort on that day was as simple as could be. Civil administration agents arrived to survey land in various places and they were always delighted to tell us that this or that block of land was state land that the villagers had poached, or land that had been purchased by a very rich and generous American Jew who tricked the Arabs and promised them he'd build a gas station on it, and they naturally didn't know he was a Jew and sold it to him. And now he wanted to transfer ownership to a *yeshivah* and so trouble might be brewing in the area. "But we of the civil administration are here only to survey the plot of land itself and pass on the maps."

On such occasions, "locals," as they were called, often materialized out of the fields or houses, wishing to present documents to the administration people or the "officer in charge," which in their jargon meant the supreme authority in the region. And then, often, some passing sergeant or one of the soldiers would present himself as the "officer in charge" in order to wave off the villager, because the real officer was busy or simply didn't feel like speaking with the Arabs. Once, "locals" showed up wishing to speak to the "officer in charge," namely myself. And they waved and showed all kinds of maps, documents, writs of ownership dating from the Ottoman Empire. The papers were colorful and decorated with official Turkish stamps, which in their opinion was ample proof of their claim to the land. The father of the family approached me. Like any other chance "officer in charge," I was not authorized to read Ottoman maps. What do I know of property laws? Perhaps I don't even know of their existence? Who even decided them? And what have they to do with me? What do I care whose land this is? What business is this of mine? After all I just need to ensure the well-being of the fellow who is here to survey this plot of land and pass the map on to whoever ordered it made and paid for it and will build whatever he will on it.

But this particular escort was not meant for surveying land, preparing a map or marking the route of future construction. The officials had come there to post paper notices on olive tree trunks. And this was the content of the notice, more or less: *This area is confiscated by the State for security purposes according to such and such regulations and by force of this and that law. Owners of the area may appeal within the time frame allowed by law to the legal authority set by the same law or regulation or edict or . . .*

I don't recall the exact words, of course, but I do remember that even then it seemed ridiculous to post such notices on the trunks of centuries-old olive trees that did not speak Hebrew, and anyway they had been planted there long before laws and regulations and edicts had been issued in Hebrew in this country, at least this time around, and if an olive tree were found that was old enough to understand, its owner certainly wouldn't, and even if he did, he would not be allowed to cross the checkpoint in order to appeal to the proper legal authority. At any rate, the official, wearing sandals, jeans and a light striped shirt, looking so out of place in this dusty landscape, took out a camera and photographed the grove and the trees with the notices posted on their trunks.

Then we escorted the civil administration vehicle to the main road. This time we passed through the village itself and not through the barrier. I don't remember the reason for changing our route, perhaps the road was especially rough and dangerous because it had not yet been completed. For some reason, I recall stopping on our way, at the village outskirts, where I opened the Jeep door and "stormily" disembarked— and here, my little thief, I must digress: the term "stormy disembarkation" is etched in my memory ever since my Jeep appeared on Israeli television news. It was in Ramallah's city center that we once stopped TV reporter Uri Levy and his film crew. This was during Operation "Onward Determination," or perhaps it was Operation "Here's to You"—one of the two. I yelled at Uri Levy that "this is a closed military zone," and we had our hands full as it was, chasing foreign television networks and we didn't really have time to waste on Israeli TV crews. He was startled, and said they had already received orders to clear out and were on their way when we stopped them. Later, when he calmed down, he smiled and complimented us on our "stormy disembarkation." I very much hoped it would be broadcast on the news, because I found it very impressive indeed.

Back at the village outskirts, I remember very well a group of children playing, and you among them, my little thief. When I saw you, with your face totally engrossed in the game, I gave you a "charming smile." Not a romantic one, the smile of the youth movement counselor—rather, a sweet but serious smile, an attempt to relay the following message: "I am sensitive but also masculine and strong."

Mere seconds had passed since the "stormy disembarkation," my look at you with the right kind of smile, and then my running off to continue our mission. But I knew myself for quite a few years by then, and I knew exactly what kind of mask I had on for every one of those seconds. After all, these were the very seconds during which you stole my Holocaust.

You did not smile back at me as had been the custom ever since I acquired that smile as a youth movement counselor. No, you froze on the spot, grew very pale and looked terrified. You neither screamed nor ran off. You only stood there, facing me with a horrified face and your black eyes staring. Normally,

I don't remember the eye color of my interlocutors and acquaintances. This is an important detail in a person's description, but when I have no intention of describing them, I don't commit their eye color to memory. But I do have a precise recollection of your eyes and their color, and I will forever.

The rest of the children ran off immediately, some crying, others generating the same hubbub that had resonated throughout their playing before we cut it off with our arrival. Only you waited there, staring at me for another shuddering moment. Then you shook yourself out of your frozen stance, turned silently—a scrawny girl in light-colored clothes—and ran off, not looking back. You ran and disappeared among the olive trees, appeared again, and then disappeared into the village alleys, forever.

And I don't know why, of all people, it was you who stole my Holocaust. After all, there was also the shackled kid in the Jeep and the girl whose family home we had broken into late at night to remove her mother and aunt. And there were plenty of children, hundreds of them, screaming and crying as we rummaged through their rooms and their things. And there was the child from Jenin whose wall we blasted with an explosive charge that blew a hole just a few centimeters from his head. Miraculously, he was uninjured, but I'm sure his hearing and his mind were badly impaired.

And there were the elderly women who had difficulty walking and we still made them march from one side of the checkpoint to the other and stand in the crowded line and wait like everyone else. And there were the proud men who suddenly broke down and wept, and the children who watched their father, the head of their family, second only to God—looking through the tears and seeing him being shackled and blindfolded and removed from his home, thrown into the Jeep. There were thousands, most of them chosen at random only because on our map their home was marked with an X.

Later, when we were sent on "massive arrest missions," as these were officially called, we no longer marked maps with Xs but simply arrested everyone—all the boys and men between fifteen and fifty-five years of age. They were detained, shackled and blindfolded. Sometimes they would be stripped, sometimes taken out of bed in pajamas and into the street. We would pass from house to house, boring holes in the walls and entering through them. We would take out the man of the house and his older children—in front of the whole family, petrified with fear—and concentrate them in groups outside.

Nowadays, whenever I see a blind person in some city walking along or waiting to cross at a pedestrian crossing, I recognize that special gait and stance, leaning forward slightly, of our detainees who would wait, blindfolded, for the truck to drive them to the interrogation facilities.

On one of our missions, I was the one who collected hundreds of detainees from the refugee camp Nur al-Shams in Bethlehem and moved them to an improvised holding pen between "curlies" in the fields of the Israeli village Nitzanei Oz. I was riding in a small military lorry, and behind us was a Safari, a large, heavy, armored personnel carrier. Both vehicles were filled with detainees, the first batch of whom were beaten up as they were unloaded into a pen by the military police-men. In response, I got off the truck and went berserk, jumping at one of the soldiers who raised a hand to my shackled detain-ees. I gripped him by the collar and shook him with great force. I yelled that if anyone here dared to hit someone again, I'd personally break his bones and send him to jail.

I spent minutes looking for the commander of the soldiers to make him watch them, but I couldn't find him and was running out of time. I couldn't wait any longer without damag-ing my vanity as the best urban navigator in my battalion. I was already being rushed on radio by company commanders who wished to rid themselves of more and more "packages"—that's what the locals are called when they are shackled and waiting to be transported into custody. I threatened the military police-men once more, perhaps added some curse, and left my detainees there.

I led the convoy back to pick up the second round, and felt that I was definitely a humane officer, one who even protected terrorists. An officer of the most moral army in the world . . . The most moral army in the world . . . The most moral . . . *Lucky for them I am here . . . Lucky that people like me . . . Fortunately it is I who do this job and not someone else, good that I . . .*

I don't know why you, of all people, and why in that village of all places . . . ? After all, there were also the students, more or less my age, facing me without lowering their gaze as the rest did, but rather looking at me straight in the eye and asking, some of them in perfect English: "How could you be so mean? Where does this meanness come from?"

Mean? Me?? No, I am not mean. I have a sense of belonging to the State. I have loyalty, sometimes compassion, lots of fear, and a lot of love and longing for a better future. I feel optimism and hope for real peace, that we shall know how to divide the country and its treasures among all humans living here—that is how I answered myself when one student, who was not allowed to cross the checkpoint to get to the university on the other side and make it in time for her final exam, faced me. Why wasn't she allowed to cross? Because that day the checkpoint was sealed shut. When would it open? I don't know. Either it would or it wouldn't.

And that student, what guts she had to stand up to me, without looking away, without lowering her gaze, without pleading, without asking me to make an exception just for her. She told me instead, in a restrained, controlled tone, as one human being to another, how much I make her and her friends suffer when I block them on their way to their final exams. That must have been no less important to her than her pride. How beautiful she was, I thought.

But she did not steal anything from me; rather, I admired her. Her and the few like her who faced me with their heads high, holding on to their own truth even at the price of relinquishing their livelihoods, their studies, their families.

CHAPTER 9

I understood only much later what that scrawny girl in light-colored clothes had taken from me: she took away my belief that there is absolute evil in the world. She took from me the belief that I was avenging my people's destruction by absolute evil, that I was fighting absolute evil. For that girl, I embodied absolute evil. Even if I was not as cruel as the absolute—Nazi—evil in the shadow of which I had grown up, I didn't have to achieve its perfection and force in order to fulfill my role in her life. No. I was merely who I was, playing the role of absolute evil in the play of her life. As soon as I realized the fact that in her eyes I myself was absolute evil, the absolute evil that had governed me until then began to disintegrate.

And ever since, I have been without my Holocaust. Ever since, everything in my life has taken on new meaning: the sense of belonging is blurred, pride has gone missing, belief has weakened, regret has grown strong, forgiveness has been born.

CHAPTER 10

At the end of my military service I was sent to the United States, and reaped tears there, too, this time in order to turn them into foreign currency, so necessary to continue building the nation and the land. Over time I have suppressed the story of that trip to such an extent that at moments I can hardly believe the words I write. Luckily, my parents have kept picture albums and newspaper clippings, proving that this was no figment of my imagination—that I was in fact sent to Miami on behalf of the IDF and Israel Bonds to tell tales of courage. This was an extreme in my life, just like the point on a mathematical function that may be seen as both the lowest trough or the highest peak, depending on the eye of the beholder. In any case, this was the point where the direction of things essentially shifted. The time that followed can be described either as a sobering elevation or as a deterioration, as humanist insight or treason. One thing is obvious though: my own picture begins to warp because memory delivers dark things it had previously suppressed. My life was a simple oil painting in which a small child is seen near a house and flowers against a neat, clear background, until someone added layers of paint that blur the clean lines. Lines blur and other lines come into focus, new victims enter my picture. Gradually, I begin to see another truth, which no longer contains my Holocaust.

Everything began by chance: a letter that my battalion adjutant, about to finish her service, received. I was out of cigarettes and knew that if I went to her office for a chat, I could share some of her Winston Lights. She said she was just reading a letter inviting an officer or two from our battalion who spoke good English to give some talks in the United States.

"How's your English?" asked the battalion commander, who came in at that moment and stood behind her.

"Just like my Hebrew," I answered with typical arrogant exaggeration.

I was then summoned for a selection day in Tel Aviv. I nearly missed it, because as chance would have it, the siege on the Muq'ata'a had been lifted that day and Israeli forces had withdrawn from Ramallah, my own battalion among them. Tired, dusty, greasy and bearded, I got out of my armored vehicle and into the company commander's Toyota and drove in a daze from occupied Ramallah to fun-loving Tel Aviv.

Outings from the madness of Bethlehem, Ramallah and the "Jerusalem wrap"—that is how we soldiers were taught to call the Arab villages north and south of the capital—were not a rare occasion for me at the time. Sometimes I would complete my tasks by 10 p.m. and leave. I always made sure that I started my trip out of the occupied territories by quarter to ten at the latest, because safety regulations required the approval of the deputy battalion commander for any movement of a civilian license-plated vehicle past 10 o'clock at night. For such approval, the trip needed to be proven necessary and the driver sufficiently fresh.

In that extra quarter of an hour, however, I would manage to get to the main road, where there was no longer any fear of running into the authorities, and drive on to a sweetheart's home, tired, happy and arrogant. There I'd shower, drink something, sleep with her, and the next morning, at 6:30, after an hour and a half of driving in "automatic pilot" mode, eyes half-shut, I'd be back on the base. When you're considered a talented officer—whether justly or because you're a good actor—and you have some friends who owe you one, you can snatch some sex, booze and freedom here and there. The price of such stolen "leave" is the problem of functioning rationally for two days straight without proper sleep, and if some mission comes up the next night, or an arrest or "show of presence," one might have to stay awake through that as well.

On such a night the world begins to fog out. One becomes particularly indifferent or, alternately, high-strung for no special reason, reckless and ruthless. Fear mixed with endless fatigue turns into a kind of drug that partially detaches one from one's surrounding and suspends inhibitions. For me this was a kind of drifting in which everything happened more slowly. The images projected from eyes to brain were as sharp as ever but my thoughts would wander and could not seem to focus. I would scold myself: *Concentrate! Wake up! Focus!* But the film remained out of sync, and at times the screen blacked out completely. It grew dark, then dimly lit, dark again, lit.

I would not know how many seconds had gone by, although outwardly I seemed to function as usual. I ran, issued commands, observed, navigated, and planned an alternative route, but my mind switched off for moments, disconnecting me from myself.

This was the same, too, for a soldier at a checkpoint or army post—for example, in the middle of a street in Hebron doing "eight-eight" shifts. These consisted of eight hours on duty and eight hours for everything else: an army meal, gear parade, weapon cleaning, cleanup at the post, phone call to Mom or girlfriend, shower, short nap, briefing for the next shift, and up to the post again for another eight hours of boredom and despair. As time went by, fatigue and exhaustion defeated common sense and morality, until one turned into an indifferent or raging machine, depending on the soldier's genetic programming and perhaps his education, a machine detached from reason and human will.

On that day, operations around the Muq'ata'a halted and I drove from Ramallah to Tel Aviv for the selection interview by the IDF spokesperson unit. I entered a noisy, crowded bureau full of officers, teeming like an anthill trampled by a heavy boot, everyone scurrying around in disarray. There were the other selection candidates. There were majors and lieutenant colonels in pressed uniforms stretched over their paunches, and quite a few junior officers like me. The line was not moving.

I even saw Johnnie there. No infantryman has failed to hear of this clown. He was frequently sent to lecture at basic training camps and officer courses, where he always drew his ancient, long, silver revolver out of his trouser belt, like some cowboy out of an American Western. His role was to promote marksmanship in the IDF. His department produced targets and marksmanship training techniques.

Johnnie was a native English speaker, with a heavy American accent in his Hebrew. He strutted and put on airs, as if he had invented the bullet and stood at Marco Polo's side in China when gunpowder first reached Western hands. Still, he deigned to enlist in our own little army. But instead of making him a legendary fighter, the army stuck him in some training department far from the front because he really knew how to train soldiers to shoot accurately. So that instead of killing Arabs with an average of some tens-of-thousands of bullets, as we did in the Yom Kippur War (when Johnnie was still galloping through the Wild West), we kill them with just a few hundred.

I really admired Johnnie's professionalism, but I also felt sorry for him, just as I felt sorry for any man back then, who did not fulfill his macho fighter dream and found himself doing good work in second-rate jobs instead.

Nowadays, I would change places with any marksmanship

instructor or safety official, with any paper-pusher and office jerk and asthmatic and junkie and anarchist and refuser. But back then I still had my Holocaust in my veins: I was a proud fighter and believed in the cause. I waited for that interview and intended to show that I was worthy of promoting that cause worldwide.

Johnnie was only one of many senior officers summoned to be interviewed, and they very much shook the self-confidence of the junior officers. We didn't think we would ever be allowed to take part in this show. Apparently, the interviewers didn't expect such a large turnout and proposed an additional day. I was so exhausted by then that I fell into a deep sleep in one of the easy chairs. Opening my eyes a while later, I realized nothing had changed. I got up and went into one of the rooms and gave one of the female soldiers my mobile phone number, asking her to call me if they wished to interview me.

I left the building, wolfed down a falafel and wandered about town. When they called me, I had already given up on the whole idea and was taking a warrior's nap on the wintry beach. But I got up immediately, proud of the greasy stains and sand on my fatigues, and proceeded to the interview.

At the end of the interview it was obvious I was chosen to go, and all those senior officers with their paunches inflated my ego even more, full to bursting. In the room sat two female officers from the IDF spokesperson unit, who explained that this mission was initiated by Israel Bonds with the purpose of selling bonds to raise funds for the State treasury. I had no clear idea what those bonds were but I imagined this meant money.

The date of the mission was unknown yet, and the officers were not sure it would even take place, but it already had a name: "Operation Maccabi."

The first question—and, if I remember correctly, the only question—I was asked after discussing my personal information was: "How would you explain the operation now taking place in Ramallah? Why did we have to lay siege to the Muq'ata'a?"

I leaned back, took a deep breath and gave such a speech . . .

The only part missing was the military master of ceremonies who would introduce me by announcing: "Will the audience please stand up, officers and NCOs in uniform—caps on and salute."

"Look, first of all I apologize for my filthy clothes and possible stench," I began, although a few hours earlier I had taken a shower at my aunt's house. "I just came here this morning straight from Ramallah. If the siege were not lifted I could not have come to this interview. The reason for attacking the Muq'ata'a is obvious. Many wanted men have taken shelter in an office building right next to Arafat's bureau. We planned to get there and blow up the bridge between that building and Arafat's offices in order to arrest the wanted men without actually harming the leader of the Palestinian Authority.

"The problem was that the bridge itself was filled with those wanted men as well as possible others. Therefore, we—for humanitarian reasons—did not wish to harm them. Those murderers and criminals, who have a lot of blood on their hands, ran along the bridge to hide behind the body of their leader himself, and thus save their souls. Such cowards. Instead of coming out and fighting they hide when we appear, and when the army turns its back they immediately send terrorists out to attack civilians. They take advantage of our kindness and our unwillingness to have the PA collapse.

"The only way to avoid hurting its leader, in spite of the fact that he knowingly protects wanted men and criminals, is to lay siege to his office until they leave. Since there was fighting in the area and we didn't want internationals to get hurt, and because of our sincere will to protect them, we did not let anyone through and declared it a closed military zone.

"As soon as the European reporters were prevented from entering the area, they were fed rumors by the Palestinians, of course, instead of inquiring with official sources such as the IDF spokesperson or some senior commander on the ground, who would immediately tell them the truth. These rumors have circulated widely in the media and created the feeling that we have something to hide, so things have tangled up even more.

"This is how pressure was built to make us partially retreat, naturally in order to return, because we shall have to arrest the killers. You see, it's exactly as in Jenin, where I also took part in the fighting during Operation Defensive Shield. They spread lies, and we—all we ask of the media is a bit of time to find out the truth and bring it out—are cornered. This is the main problem when you fight terrorism within a civilian population and are also responsible for the well-being of internationals and innocents in the area.

"Look," I turned to the senior interviewer. "The

information problem in such warfare is unavoidable and we have to look for creative solutions in order to bring out the simple truth of our war." I then proceeded with stories and heroic tales of arrest missions that went wrong and the Palestinians' ingratitude, as on the one hand they hide terrorists, and on the other they hurry to publicize any accidental damage we cause.

The two officers smiled and exchanged glances, and the senior one said: "Finally a real answer from someone on the ground who also understands the greater picture."

If another single drop of ego were fed into my veins, all the falafel I'd eaten plus a large bottle of grapefruit juice would have had to be sucked out to make room for my growing self-love, and my assurance of the justice of my cause, our cause.

What I didn't tell those interviewers is that all of those stories—about the Muq'ata'a and the bridge and the terrorists—I learned only from rumors originating in the units that were actually inside, from partial listening to the brigade's radio net and the news I heard on the way to the interview, in which the IDF spokesperson was quoted as usual. Beyond that, I didn't tell, and I suppose they were not interested in hearing, about all the things I simply had not seen and didn't know until I lost my Holocaust and they suddenly became visible, memorable, conscious.

I didn't tell them that our APCs and tanks and bulldozers entered Ramallah—a handsome, modern city, even impressive—and crushed and destroyed private and public property while grinding to dust any part of the town's infrastructure which they happened to run across. Sidewalks and roads and bus stops, traffic dividers and road signs, public parks and drainage ditches, telephone poles, playgrounds and decorative trees, hedges and stone walls—everything was pulverized and smashed to smithereens like sandcastles on the beach. Nor did I tell them how our heavy equipment crushed cars at roadsides, sometimes with barely disguised pleasure, sometimes by mistake, sometimes with regret that there was no other option. No one, however, left a note under a windshield wiper: *Sorry I trampled your car, call the IDF.* In most cases no windshield wipers were left anyway in the mess of metal and broken glass that had once been a family vehicle.

Nor did I tell them that bulldozers moving through narrow alleyways sometimes ripped off sections of house walls that consequently become open lattices. I didn't tell them that the regional brigade commander opened live fire—in violation of his own official orders, incidentally—at a demonstration that was taking place 300 meters from us up the Muq'ata'a road. This shooting stunned us and surprised even our legendary battalion commander. I didn't tell them how the demonstrators who ran away later came back with Molotov cocktails and burning wooden wheels and threw stones, and how a line of Border Patrolmen dispersed this demonstration with more live fire, teargas and beatings.

The clothes of the detainees in the Border Patrol Jeeps were drenched with blood, because all of them, when trying to run off, "fell with their faces on the asphalt." That's the explanation on the medical report because under our enlightened occupation, every detainee sees a doctor to whom you have to account for the wounds. *Can't just go ahead and beat them up, order must prevail!* I didn't tell them that I detained Red Cross ambulances and had no idea what rights the Red Cross had in our area or in the world, and when some Englishman raged at me saying he was a pacifist and had never held a gun in his life and what gall I had to search for weapons in his ambulance, I only smiled and thought how naïve of him not to realize they might take advantage of his naiveté, and proceeded to rummage through every medication cabinet and everywhere else in his vehicle.

Nor did I tell them that, sometimes, in order to have a safe night's rest, we would choose some chance house and enter, locking up the whole family in one small room and settling down in the rest of the house. And that we preferred comfortable, heated homes, with the excuse that the house of our choice was the safest. Nor did I describe to them what such a residence looked like after twenty men, filthy with dust and mud, lived in it and did in it as they very well pleased. And what the couches or rugs in the living room looked like, especially the rugs, after they were lifted up and nailed to the wall over the windows for blackout purposes, so no one would be able to look and take a shot inside. Or what a beautiful wooden desk looked like when sandbags were loaded on it and how a bedroom looked after serving as a fortified position. If I had told them these things, the interviewers would have been able to imagine what their own private bathrooms and toilets would have looked like if twenty-odd chaps were to turn them into public latrines. But I had no reason in the world to include stinking details in my hero's tale.

Nor did I describe feelings, for I never took too much trouble to look into them until I lost my Holocaust. I didn't wonder how a soldier felt when I ordered him to guard a door behind which a whole family was locked, such that the family members had to ask his permission to go to the toilet. What did he feel? How was he supposed to feel when he could not let the lady of the house go to the kitchen because we were just then unpacking some technical system she was not supposed to see? And anyway she had taken food out of there, that fat Arab lady; how much do they actually need to eat?

I don't know what was better for such a family, but sometimes we, our company, sent the family away instead of locking them up in one of the rooms. I let them have an hour to pack their necessaries and leave. I told them to watch the house from a distance and wait for the day when our APCs were no longer parked out front; then they'd know they could come back home. At first I would even point out a spot from which a certain family member could wave to us and we'd let him come and pick up stuff they needed. Back then I still tried to leave the house clean and neat. Sometimes we even washed the floor before we left. I ordered the men not to use electricity, food or furniture, because we were "the most moral army in the world" . . .

That mantra was always repeated to us, enabling us to detach ourselves from reality. And that is how we repeated it to our own subordinates. But as occupying houses became a matter of routine, the number of "moral" orders dwindled. After we moved from house to house through holes bored in the walls, after we smashed doors and closets and tiles and tore up couches and chairs in search of wanted men and ammunition, it no longer made sense to order the men "don't sit on the couches" in the next house.

After sending a soldier to smash up a desk and the bookshelves above it, it was hard to be angry at him for taking pleasure in smashing the living-room television set as well. And I still yelled: "Why did you do this, what's the point?" But he was a strong fellow, perhaps the only one of my exhausted men who still had the energy to wave the heavy hammer at the end of a long night of "house-to-house searches" in the Jenin refugee camp. Returning to our battalion headquarters after the operation, I demanded of the battalion commander that he try the soldier for the superfluous destruction of that television set. The commander placed a paternal hand on my shoulder and suggested I take a walk around the base with him.

"If you wish," he told me, "I'll try him and give him any punishment you choose, but I suggest you consider the extenuating circumstances. Think about what he has been through in this operation. Besides, it has been three weeks since he broke that television set and time is also on his side."

The chap was neither tried nor punished. Today, I am glad I let him alone and didn't deny him his precious leave. For after all, no one had punished me for the perforated house walls and furniture broken at my command, no one punished my superior for the whole houses he destroyed and no one punished his superior for whole city infrastructures and olive groves that he sent us to destroy and uproot. At any rate, later we didn't even see the private property of the home owners we had invaded. We simply placed ourselves in them as comfortably as possible, sometimes for a single night, sometimes for weeks on end.

CHAPTER 11

But I shall never forget my first house. The two women and the girl whom we threw out of their home compete in my mind even with the girl who stole my Holocaust over the power of memory and pain. It was during the occupation of the city of Tul Karm.

Before we entered the town, the battalion commander gathered the troops. It was no simple feat to get all the companies together to the very last man, for we were up to our necks in preparations for the operation and had gone for days without proper sleep. The commander began by proudly announcing that this was the first time a city was going to be occupied in the present confrontation and that this important mission has been assigned to our Nahal brigade, reinforced by a tank battalion and other auxiliaries.

Then he made some lofty, hollow remarks about the objectives of this ruthless operation and finally proceeded to describe the dangers that army intelligence had reported, as it were: there would be explosive charges hanging from power lines and scattered on the roads. House doors would be booby-trapped, snipers waiting for us behind every corner, and "it is highly likely," he said with open, excited pleasure, "that some of you will end up smelling the flowers from underneath." He added that "one should be prepared for the eventuality that in war people die. You are soldiers and soldiers are the people whom society sometimes sends off to die."

At first I was moved and appreciated him for his frankness and courage, but I left this assembly very scared, and overly alert. I wanted to bring my men back alive, all of them, and this thought wouldn't let up for a moment. I anticipated encountering volleys of gunfire and blasting mines and simply forgot that we were in fact entering a city. Compared to the briefing given by my company commander before entering Jenin, this one was gentle. That other briefing contained merely seven words: "Guys, we're gonna fuck them. Get moving!"

I received the mission from my superior about half an hour before leaving.

I commanded a platoon of young soldiers, *yeshivah* students, and this was our first serious assignment, not counting the vendetta we had carried out against the cave dwellers in the South Hebron Hills following the murder of a Jewish settler there, or the smaller vendetta we carried out in the same area against tent dwellers following the loss of a mortar that fell off our Jeep while driving. We had to establish that it had been stolen by Palestinians living near our basic training camp and carried out searches and toppled encampments and chased off flocks, until someone in command relaxed in his air-conditioned office.

Tul Karm was my first assignment as platoon commander. I was in charge of three APCs and a tank. The tank commander was a pale-looking fellow, so scared that at certain moments I felt pity for him. But mostly contempt. He came to us a few days earlier from tank commanders' training and had never led a mission. Unlike me, he had also never served as a soldier on any military mission of any kind. He wouldn't drive without ground navigators' assistance, unwilling to move until a bulldozer had arrived to make sure there were no mines, and demanded we turn on lights to show him the way. He needed time to study the route and did not follow me as I navigated. "I need to understand where I'm going," he said.

With this guy on board everything I'd ever been told about the Armor Corps suddenly became true: he was hard headed. My company commander at the time was a high-strung icebox, about five feet tall, three feet deep and three feet wide, and always nervous. He gripped the tank commander by the shirt, shook him and said: "Listen! This is your superior, now do what he says, and from now on, you shut up." The fellow shut up, calmed down, and when we came to a house and spent a few days inside, he turned out to be a very nice hard-head who cared for his soldiers and usually did what he was told and kept quiet.

Our assignment was to enter some village on a hill next to the town and take one of the "strategic" houses—namely, a house located high enough to afford a good lookout over the town, so that we could provide information in real time to the forces taking over the town center below. It might sound like a serious assignment but in hindsight it proved to be bullshit. We drove to the village and climbed to the highest point, where I faced my first dilemma.

On the designated road was a high-rise building still under construction, a skeleton. No one inhabited it yet. Next door stood several tall and handsome houses, which must have belonged to wealthy locals. It seemed the right thing to do, enter a house under construction because there were no dwellers inside and no resistance anticipated. On the other hand, I thought, we would be very uncomfortable and cold in such an exposed structure. This consideration, based as it was on soldier security and safety, had the upper hand. I chose the tallest and handsomest house on the street.

The battalion commander had promised us explosive charges and booby-traps wherever we turned. Now, after having entered hundreds of houses during my time in the army, this scenario seems to me absolute fiction, even surreal. But back then, it made sense. Why shouldn't there be resistance? So I decided to enter the tall and handsome house in a way that would make the people inside understand that they only stood to lose if they resisted. The house was on pillars, with all of the rooms on the second story. A small porch with a large glass door looked upon the street. I sent the tank to stand under the house and turn its cannon directly at the glass door. The tip of the barrel reached a few meters from the entrance. I sent sentries in pairs to surround the house in case anyone tried to get away. This was the standard procedure before sending a neighbor or a passer-by to knock on the door, after which we would want to remove our suspects.

I did not stop to think that this was just a random residence that we were going to take over in the middle of the night. After the tank cannon had been positioned and the soldiers had surrounded the house, we began to make noise. We drove one of the APCs back and forth and yelled until a light was turned on in the window facing the tank. We saw a figure looking out the window and heard a woman yelling inside. When we were sure that the enemy had comprehended the fire power we might use, we ascended the outer concrete stairway to the entrance. I took the two tallest soldiers I had. One held a machine gun and had night vision equipment on his helmet—because it all looked very scary—and the other carried a weapon with telescopic sights.

When entering houses like this one, I preferred to have one soldier carry a machine gun and the other an axe or five-kilo hammer, which is more frightening and opens doors faster than any home owner, as welcoming as he may be. I banged on the door and yelled "Open up, army!" in my thickest, angriest voice. The door opened and a woman in her forties stood facing me. Behind me something crashed; one of the soldiers had tripped against a ceramic flowerpot and it fell down the rail-less stairwell and broke against the concrete floor in the yard. The woman wore a thick red nightgown with a rather low neckline. I recall a plump but strong-looking woman, with a round face and short neck. When she saw the three of us standing in front of her at the doorway, she was startled. She gave a short scream and jumped back, her hand covering her mouth. We entered the house, behind us another few soldiers, aiming our weapons in all directions.

"Where's your husband?"

"In Kuwait."

"What, Kuwait, who's in Kuwait!" one of the soldiers yelled. "Probably fighting together with all his buddies downtown, her terrorist!" This idea heightened our sense of mission and alertness.

"Everyone in this house get down here immediately!" I ordered as I began to send more and more soldiers inside. Another woman, older and less attractive, came out of one of the rooms and wept. We lowered our guns slowly and told her to calm down. The first woman went to get her daughter from the other room. We were dealing here with two sisters or perhaps a woman and her mother-in-law, and the daughter of the first woman, a twelve-year-old girl, also wearing a similar though lighter nightgown of some faded orange color. She was a plump girl with quite a few pimples on her forehead, braces on her teeth and a frightened look in her eyes.

I sent two soldiers to check all the rooms and make sure there was no one else in the house. When the search was over we relaxed, and thereafter everything was calmer. I pointed at the large clock hanging in the living room, which read a quarten past midnight. I told them they had one hour to pack everything they needed and "get going."

The mother looked at me in disbelief. I repeated the instruction in Hebrew spiked with Arabic, a jargon that, when I eventually opened my eyes, I called "Occupationese." It had no extensive vocabulary; it was short, blunt and to the point. Most words were conjugated in the imperative: *Close! Get in! Open! Go! Hands up! Get your husband! Shut up!* There are a few more expressions, such as: *Whoever throws a stone will be punished! I'm not your friend!* There are also naturalized Hebrew words: *machsom* (checkpoint), *magav* (Border Patrol Police), *chayalim* (soldiers), *katzin* (officer in charge), *tank* (tank) . . .

The mother understood. She came to her senses and asked, "For how long?" I said one week; perhaps a month. The truth was I had no idea. She grew pale, got a hold of herself again and began to give instructions and pack things. First she went to the kitchen and poured whatever was in the pots into plastic containers. Then she packed clothes, sheets, blankets. Gunfire resounded in town and the older woman began to cry again. I tried to smile. She wouldn't look at me. The tank commander came upstairs to the apartment and said that downstairs, next to the house, was a good spot to place the tank, with a good lookout over the city center. I sent him to do just that and sent the APC drivers to park them facing the road.

Meanwhile, the older woman calmed down. The mother packed and yelled words I couldn't understand in Arabic to her daughter, who was sent to pack. When the tank began to move under the house, its chains creaking and crushing the garden and fruit trees under the window of her room, it was the daughter's turn to burst into tears. Her mother yelled at her, calmed her down and continued packing, covering the sofas and moving furniture in the bedroom.

Towards one o'clock in the morning, all three were at the house door ready to leave. From down the hill faint gunfire was still heard. I had no idea what was going on down there and no one answered me on the radio except the war room, to which forces on the ground were supposed to report information. I reported that we were positioned, beginning to fortify ourselves and would soon begin to report. Report what, I didn't know. Nor to whom.

The mother asked the girl something before leaving, and the girl answered "no" and stamped her feet. The mother made me understand that she didn't want to take her schoolbooks with her. The girl pointed down at the town, where gunfire resounded, as if stating: *it's a war, who needs schoolbooks now?* The mother and girl looked at me, each wanting me to support her point of view. The girl's face was swollen with tears. I looked helplessly at the mother, then at the girl and again at the mother. The mother looked at me and smiled all of a sudden; she was the first to realize how ridiculous that moment was. I smiled, too, and then the girl cracked up laughing, choking through her tears. I took off my helmet and nodded, sent her to her room to get her schoolbooks.

I tried to promise the mother that we wouldn't hurt the house. I don't think she understood. "When these will no longer be outside," I said pointing to the APCs, "you will come back home." The girl reappeared with her school bag packed full. I addressed the mother again, pointing at a large bush and said that if she had forgotten anything, she could stand there and wave and I would tell her to approach. She nodded, and urged her daughter and sister or mother-in-law to leave.

They left and I never saw them again, except in my waking nightmares. I often saw their faces when I imagined the scene taking place at my parents' house, at homes of my childhood friends and neighbors, at the home of my girlfriend's parents and even in many homes where I have only once been a guest. How would the lady of the house have functioned? How would her daughter or son have reacted?

As a man, I couldn't avoid thinking of the husband. How did he feel when he heard about this in Kuwait or when he came back from fighting in the town? What did he feel knowing he could not be there to protect his wife, daughter, sister-in-law or mother? How did he deal with this humiliation, with this kind of helplessness? And how would I have responded, finding out that a group of strange men made my wife and daughter get out of bed in the middle of the night and threw them out into the street? What would I feel when asking myself what looks they got? What were they wearing? What additional pain were they withholding from me? Did anything else happen to them? What kind of a memory does that girl carry from that moment when a bearded Israeli officer took off his helmet and nodded her back to her room so she wouldn't miss school on account of the war?

But these wimpy, aching thoughts would only cross my mind when I no longer possessed my Holocaust. Back then, in that village not far from Tul Karm, they didn't. I was busy just doing my job.

"What the hell are we doing here?" one of the soldiers eventually asked. And we really did nothing. For the first few hours we were busy securing the house: we covered the windows with curtains and rugs, brought up sand bags from the APCs and set up observation and sniper posts at the windows. We assigned each other guard duty shifts, I wrote down post procedures and we began to guard ourselves, preparing food and sleeping in turns.

We tried to "lookout" over the town, but the distance was too great for our simple sighting devices. The tank crew could see a narrow slice of the goings-on there, but we didn't know where our forces were or what their assignments were. So even if we noticed anything relevant, we wouldn't know whom to report it to. We tried to ask a few times, and when we realized that no one was interested in us, I asked permission to leave the spot. Headquarters wouldn't give it, but sparing our feelings, I guess, they changed our assignment: no longer an observation force, we were now a reserve crew—unreasonable drivel in itself, for as reserves we could have stayed at a rear base, closer to the city entrance and not closed up and awkward inside the village. I passed on the message to the soldiers verbatim, not sharing with them my bitterness for sitting there idle. The next day I asked to leave, and was again refused.

A few days later, when the forces below in the town began to exit, we were finally ordered to get back to base. One of the APCs would not start and we had to wait for a rescue team to come fix it. The company commander arrived in his armored Jeep and led away the two working APCs and the tank. I remained in the village for another day with a small force and the broken-down APC. Anyone going out into the street while we were there was yelled at and threatened back indoors. No one dared get close to us. More long hours went by until the rescue team arrived, and then we got out.

As we were the last force to leave, a gang of boys threw stones at us. A large stone hit the APC roof. I had my head out and was startled. I closed the top and bent down inside. My sudden entry disconnected the communication wire that enabled me to speak to the driver. He was startled by the noise and when I didn't answer, looked back at me — "to make sure you weren't hurt," he explained the next day — while pulling the right hand stick.

The APC skidded sideways and ran over a parked car. It was a beautiful black VW "bug" with an antique hood and front grill, a real gem that someone had groomed and pampered. Our right-hand chain climbed over the car and crushed it softly like a chocolate delicacy between teeth. And then we drove on. The deputy battalion commander who passed by the car after us commented to me the next day: "I saw you did a nice job on some collectors' item." I began to describe the incident but he interrupted me with half a smile and a wink, saying, "Accidents happen, old chap. You have nothing to apologize about. It's alright."

It didn't feel right to know he thought I did it on purpose, but only a very long time later, orphaned of my Holocaust, and without my feeling of absolute righteousness, would I realize how terrible that wink was.

CHAPTER 12

I didn't tell my interviewers at the army spokesperson's offices in Tel Aviv about our deeds in that village, nor did I reveal them to the Jews in Miami. I didn't tell them that out of sheer boredom we stole a Quran from the bookcase in that house, or that we took photos of ourselves wearing black Hassidic skullcaps under wall decorations of Arabic prayer verses, our weapons hanging on our shoulders and our fingers Victorying the way suicide bombers do before getting on their way. I didn't tell them that the number of our superfluous assignments grew and grew and even then, had I only opened my eyes, I could have understood that the main point of my being there was being there per se. Being there meant the accident with the crushed VW, the humiliation of the inhabitants of that house and the damage to its surroundings. Not on lookout duty, not as troops securing an action, certainly not carrying out any war on terror.

In Miami I repeated the same things time and again to a different audience each day: we shall pursue the terrorists wherever and whenever we shall see fit. It is our right and duty to fight terror and destroy the infrastructure of Palestinian terrorism. (I loved that expression—"the terror infrastructure"—and used it a lot when I answered questions at the end of my talk.) I mentioned the Israeli army's operation to free the hijacked French plane in Entebbe, Uganda: "Remember that the Palestine Liberation Organization terrorists, whose successors we are fighting now, freed the French passengers and sent the Jews to the left, just as the Jews had been selected by the Nazis and sent to their death in Auschwitz all those years ago. Our IDF said loud and clear: Never again! Never again will Jews be selected and sent off to die! We didn't just say it, the IDF sent forth the best recon unit to rescue them. Ladies and gentlemen, my dear hostess, rest assured that back then, as on this very day, we shall not let anyone hurt us just because we are Jews!"

And at the end of every speech, "Hatikvah" was played. Behind me was a large Israeli flag and while we played and sang the national anthem, I wore my beret over my prim dress uniform and saluted the flag. This was the highlight of the evening; the audience was moved every time. The Bonds fundraisers repeated all kinds of stories from those evenings. For example, about an American grandfather who said: "You know, my dear, every year I donate 10,000 dollars, but when I saw this young Israeli man salute the flag I decided to go double this year."

"Allow me to say a few words," the evening's fundraiser would begin, and make a few more financial comments and remind all present how lucrative investment in Israel really was, a state that had never postponed paying its debts to its investors. He would finish by saying, "Since all of you came here to hear this young veteran of the battle in Jenin who has come here especially for you . . ." Without further delay he would introduce me with the words passed on to him by the IDF spokesperson department: Lieutenant Noam Chayut, the hero of blah blah blah blah . . .

Right after my speech the audience would pose questions, which were always prefaced by long list of compliments and thanks: for your English and your blessed bravery, and you should know I have a daughter just slightly younger than you (forced, hypocritical laughter in the audience, just like in an American sitcom). And thank you from the bottom of my heart and our hearts, all of us, for having come all the way here, because it is so important for us to receive first-hand information, it is so unbearably hard to be so far away when our heart and soul are with you out there all the time, as you cope with those hardships. The first question was nearly always: What do you propose we do? Besides buying bonds, whom can we donate to? How can we help? Then several questions were asked regarding political issues, and I apologized in my scripted way that I was not allowed to answer them in the uniform that represents the entire nation with all its myriad views. Then there were personal questions, which I was always glad to answer extensively, and then "Hatikvah" with my beret and salute, and thanks, and refreshments and greetings — and on to the hotel.

Once I was even taken to a Jewish school. The fundraiser suggested that children about to be Bar-Mitzvah-ed should ask for Israel Bonds as a gift. I was presented to the kids as a war hero who has come to the US for rest and recuperation from the battles now being fought in the state that is theirs as well as ours. I added how great it was to be a soldier and a representative of our nation, and because most of them were sons of immigrant families from Cuba, I joked around with them a bit in Spanish. They laughed, especially at my accent and stammering and perhaps even at the jokes themselves.

The Bonds representative sweetly reminded them that when the rich Cubans escaped from the communist island, with many Jews among them, they were not allowed to take any money with them, nor documents or papers, and as you know, sweet children, without money one cannot really make it in our America. The Jews were lucky because many of them had Israel Bonds, and although they did not have their papers with them, and although the money was supposed to be paid only many years later, they went to the Israeli Embassy, mentioned the numbers of their bonds, and then our faraway good-hearted state, which this brave officer helped defend, immediately paid them all their money, and because of the goodness of the warm Jewish heart we were all smiling and happy. Therefore, dear children, it is important to remind your parents of this story and ask for all your gifts to be in Israel Bonds instead of dollars. Memorize the numbers of your personal Bonds certificates and this way you'll stay protected forever.

One evening I went out to a pub near my hotel and drank too much. The guy next to me at the bar wouldn't stop ordering vodkas and tequilas for me. I am a bad drinker and one glass of beer was enough for me to be happy. After the second, I began to talk nonsense, the third gave me a headache, and after the fourth I threw up. We sat at the bar, and he said my stories really moved him. When the bartender moved away from us to serve someone else, he interrupted me and said: "I don't really care about all that Middle East bullshit of yours, but I saw how thrilled *she* got" and pointed at the bartender, "and all I'm interested in is her ass and those boobs of hers" and pointed at her again. "I'm getting you drinks so she'll stay here near me, so when she's not here you can shut up." He chuckled and lit himself a cigarette. I got offended and lit one for myself as well.

The bartender was a war refugee from Yugoslavia. She had a delicately foreign accent, well-inflated silicon-implanted breasts and a tiny ass stuffed into skinny jeans. He paid for her proximity with many dollars buying drinks for me, and once in a while he'd say to her: "Did you hear his story? It's heart-rending, really. What a complicated world." She answered that luckily there are people like him who, although far away from other people's problems, at least were sensitive and attentive enough to such distress. She also told some harsh war memories of her own childhood.

The next morning, at ten o'clock, I delivered my speech and saluted the flag with a terrible hangover. The earth wouldn't stop spinning around me. The Bonds representative asked if I was alright. "Yes," I said. In the car, after a moment of silence, she told me the story of her life, including her experiences of being sexually harassed by old rich Jews, regular buyers and commission inflators. "Hang in there, young man, it's only another hour and a half. I'll try to make your day shorter and you should know I did hard drugs for a while, ecstasy and hallucinogenic mushrooms and what have you, I know what it's like to get up like this. You'll be alright."

And I really was fine: a shorter fanfare than usual, salute the flag, applause, money collection and apologies for leaving because we have another event on short notice—then ride to the hotel and sink deep into the soft bed.

CHAPTER 13

On days when I lectured to Miami Jews, I slept in fancy hotels and ate lush meals. Afternoons I'd spend swimming at a beach full of silicon breasts or at the hotel pool. I treated myself to cocktails I had never heard of, watched films in my hotel room, including some "soft porn" to relieve some of my loneliness, and drank overpriced beer out of the mini-bar. All of this, it must be admitted, was paid for by the Israeli taxpayer. My pocket still contained the 500 dollars that the IDF gave us for any extra expenses. It was not such a bad deal for someone who, just a week earlier, was sprawled every night on a thin army mat, asleep in fatigues and shoes, sometimes at standby, at others times simply determined to get a few more minutes of sleep.

Others from our delegation—"fourteen male and female combatants, successors of the Maccabees," as the ambassador put it—postponed their return flight to Israel and took their own planned vacation. I didn't. I had promised the adjutant's office that I would be back as soon as the mission was over to get discharged. But the moment we landed in New York, I knew I wanted to extend my stay abroad as long as possible.

In New York our delegation was presented to the Israeli ambassador and consul and community dignitaries and many government and media people at a very posh dinner in a posh hotel. The consul, or perhaps deputy ambassador or some other senior official, delivered a vivid speech and received us with pride and open delight. He spoke about the essence of Israeli *hasbara* and diplomacy and its strategic importance, especially in the United States. One of the highlights of his speech that I remember was when he explained why the word *hasbara* was difficult to translate into English.

"You must understand," he said, "*hasbara* is not just diplomacy. It does not just mean 'a description of reality.' It is much more than that. There is no English term for *hasbara*, and the verb 'to explain'—*lehasbir*—lacks the proper depth. The best definition for *hasbara* that my friend the Ambassador and I use in English is 'truth telling.'"

What a poignant punch line.

Truth telling. Yes, that's right, I told the truth in my speeches. "We shall continue to pursue terror and damage its infrastructures."

Truth or not?

Truth.

But what is the destruction of terror infrastructure, what exactly does pursuing terror mean?

I didn't know.

Who knows?

Here:

"Exposure" (razing—uprooting trees and flattening buildings);

"Targeted prevention" (extrajudicial execution);

"Show of presence" (humiliation, intimidation, vandalism);

"Neighbor procedure" (using a random unarmed bystander as a human shield in order to enter a Palestinian house);

"Passer-by procedure" (same thing, after "neighbor procedure" was ruled illegal by Israel's High Court of Justice);

"Searches" (entering homes and damaging their contents);

"Deterrent fire" (opening fire indiscriminately in all directions);

"Making them pay the price" (revenge, letting off steam and collective punishment);

"Mapping" (invading the last vestige of privacy in the refugee camps: entering every home, drawing the layout of the rooms, listing the names of the inhabitants, scanning their mobile phones, checking out family relations . . .).

And so "the Palestinian population is to learn that terrorism doesn't pay."

Truth. I did tell the truth in my speeches. I just didn't tell all of it. I didn't lie, didn't distort. I didn't even exaggerate. But I didn't tell the true story.

Between the speech of the deputy ambassador, or consul, and dessert, I left the hotel to search for a public phone in the pleasant chilly March weather in New York. I made three calls:
1. To a travel agency to reserve my ticket from Miami to Mexico

and back; 2. To the delegation's Bonds coordinator in order to extend the validity of my ticket; 3. To my battalion adjutant, which was an especially pleasant call.

True, I hadn't planned to stay abroad and travel, but like a good army man I was ready for this contingency. Since I decided not to continue my service as a company commander, my adjutant, a very nice fellow, demanded that I get discharged before my flight. I disagreed. What am I, some kind of sucker? Why should I give up nearly half a month's salary—ten days in Miami and another two days before and one day after? After all, I was in uniform all this time and following the orders of the IDF spokeswoman. "Adjutantissimo," I said, "please resolve my bureaucratic troubles with the spokesperson's bureau: as a soldier I want to be paid."

He resolved the problems but notified me that now I had to return to Israel immediately upon ending the mission and get discharged forthwith. A day before my flight I wrote a letter addressed to the battalion adjutant's office:

To Whom it May Concern,

I hereby appoint the battalion adjutant (name and serial number) or anyone on his behalf, to discharge me from the army in my absence, beginning March 18th, 2003 (three days from the end of my military duty, since I still have three days of unused leave).

Sincerely,

Lieutenant Noam Chayut, serial number 5732683

I included my soldier's certificate, sealed the envelope, and pasted on a stamp.

And this, more or less, was the third call, from New York to the adjutant's office:

"I'm not coming back."

"You must get discharged. You also have to fill out your discharge form, and return your military ID. It's impossible."

"It is possible. There's a letter on its way to you, containing . . . Listen bro, I'm running out of coins. If it doesn't work you can pay my salary until I get back. Thanks for everything and goodbye."

It worked, and that's how I was discharged not at *bakum*, but on an enchanted island beach of the coast of Belize, white sand and coral reefs all around. I was free and happy.

PART TWO

CHAPTER 14

This part of the story of the theft of my Holocaust took place in between the theft itself and the realization that something was no longer a part of me. I suppose this time lapse was necessary. It could have taken years, perhaps a lifetime, and then my story would have been one of those old men's tales told upon their deathbed. In my case, for reasons unknown to me, the revelation came sooner. This was a time of physical and mental relief from the army and life's commitments in general, a time of rest free of regret or introspection. When I write about that period of time, I seek bits of evidence and proof of the thought processes that began to change without my being aware of it. I find chronological contradictions in the plot, things I said too early, decisions I made a long time ago that were not typical of me at the time.

I had, indeed, done five whole years of regular military service and was planning to resume my life as a civilian. In Israel, however, every civilian is still a potential reserves serviceman, to be called up at any given moment either for training or for the inevitable conflagration. The childish game I played with my battalion adjutant and my sweet triumph over military red tape was to have great meaning in the future. Since I was not properly discharged at the army's conscription and discharge center, I was not screened and assigned as an officer to a future recon reserves unit. My file meandered among various offices and I would end up in the Homefront Command's rescue battalion. I would never wield a gun again. All of which would happen without my having to explain to any commission or military judge that *I cannot do this, simply cannot, my Holocaust has been stolen from me and with it, my faith in our common cause, your honor, honored commissioners, and today that noble cause of yours is no longer mine . . .*

My first reserves duty call came when not quite a year had passed since my discharge, and the summons for screening had a handwritten addendum: "volunteer day."

I had no grudge yet against the army, and was glad to cooperate. I expected to be interviewed by reserves recon unit commanders in preparation for my assignment as a team commander in one of their companies. In the waiting room, something already felt wrong. Waiting with me were only officers, both male and female, who had desk jobs in their regular service. Still, I patiently awaited my turn. A major called me in and printed my official sheet from her computer—a document listing my military rank and the marks I received in my various trainings and periodic evaluations by superiors.

"That's your name?" she asked.

"Yes."

"Serial number 5732683?"

"Yes."

"What are you doing here?"

"I don't know. This is room number ten at training base sixteen, Tzerifin. This is me, and this is where you summoned me to report in this letter a while ago, and when the IDF calls, I show up." I was quoting a famous Israeli comedian from an old Israeli film. She laughed and I thought she looked good considering her age and rank.

"Ever done drugs?"

"No, I've never smoked." This was the absolute truth at the time.

"Jail time?"

"What?"

"Criminal record?"

"No. What are all these questions?"

"Look, it says you're an infantry officer, done recon training, had super grades in squad commander and officer courses, your last commanding officer commended you as one of the pillars of your battalion, and here's a recommendation by your brigade commander to summon you to a reserves company commanders' course. It also says you refused to take on this assignment during your regular army duty in spite of your aptitude."

"Thank you, nice of them. I really did my best. So what's the story?"

"I don't understand why you've been summoned to the Home Front Command screenings."

"Neither do I," I retorted.

I was deeply disappointed, as I had prepared a blazing speech in favor of a good assignment to one of the reserves recon units. She left the office with some papers, then returned and led me to the next room. There I met my home-front battalion and company commanders. They were both elderly, volunteers, retired. They told me about the battalion's objectives and its men. "It's a normal battalion in the home-front command, not one of those considered cutting-edge and on constant standby, or doing extra reserves time. We have a much simpler job. Our job in the coming few years will consist of running patrols along the dormant borders with Jordan and Egypt."

"And if I claim my right to be a combatant or recon officer?" I asked.

They both laughed, and the senior of the two said, "You still have the mind of a regular soldier, not a reserves officer. Everything is different here. First of all, do take a few months off and clean up your military lingo. On reserves we don't struggle for a unit transfer. At most we file a request. You will not be forced to stay with us. If you so wish, you'll be transferred wherever you please. But you're not going to. You'll end up with a job, a family and will certainly first want to be a student for a few years. Your head won't be in the army."

How right he was.

CHAPTER 15

Post-army travel is a widespread Israeli practice, no less than academic studies. Perhaps more so. It usually goes on for many months and has all the symptoms of a quest for one's self free of military discipline. But it also has the symptoms of an escape. While I could have gone on traveling in Central America, I had a love in Hungary. I had met her in Israel shortly before the end of my military service but she had returned home to Hungary, knowing she wanted to try living in our country—which had also been hers until the age of six—and that she loved me very much. I came home and applied for a summer job as a counselor at a camp in Hungary for the children of Eastern Europe Jews. I was chosen for the job and enjoyed two marvelous months—a rickety wooden shack on a riverbank, green grass, good friends, cute kids, lots of beer, and a marvelous love.

At my job interview I had to answer two questions more significant than the rest: First, how did I feel about a camp that was Jewish but not necessarily Zionist? And second, did I think that my recently completed army service might impair my capacity to work with young children at a camp known for its free and easy atmosphere? I answered the first question, saying that although I was a Zionist first and a Jew second, I was willing to learn and teach and that I had strong feelings for religion, which back then was true. As for my military service, I said, "No way! In the army I was not a tough commander. After all, before my service I worked with kids as a youth movement counselor."

It was the right answer, but in hindsight it was not quite true. Like every discharged veteran, it took me a while to shed my army shell. Now I realize I was actually a very tough commander. "Head against the wall," as the saying goes. I was motivated by lofty values perhaps, but I also very closely followed my male ego. And indeed, at the camp in Hungary a group of counselors from Lithuania resented me when I scolded them for lacking a sense of leadership and for regularly showing up late in the morning. They then came dressed in black to one of the meals, marched like soldiers past my table, saluted in unison and sat at another table. Everyone laughed and I was offended.

At the same time, I was accused of being a leftie more than once at the camp, probably because of things I said about the rights of Palestinian to a certain liberty in the holy land. I have ample proof, however, that at that time I was still mostly my "former self." For example, rather than teaching the kids singing, dancing, or Jewish culture like the other counselors did, I led an "army class." In my class, Russian, Ukrainian, Yugoslav, Serbian, Croatian, Hungarian, Rumanian, Bulgarian and other children wore IDF uniforms, some of which I had brought with me from Israel. I led them in drills around the camp as they yelled "Sir, yes sir!" in various accents. They practiced wrestling and fending off stabbers, did sit-ups and push-ups, and in our last meeting we all ran together to the pool, tore off our uniforms and jumped into the water.

But even then I did not use that scene—as I might do nowadays—as the basis for the dream that someday we would all take off our uniforms and live in peace with our neighbors. True, that class was not my own initiative but part of the usual camp curriculum, but today I certainly wouldn't choose to lead it. When I now introduce myself as an Israeli in India or elsewhere, and inevitably someone says, "Wow, Mossad . . ." or "How strong a country you are," I am ashamed to belong to a place associated first and foremost with force—not sanctity, nor wisdom, nor even money—just brute force.

My memory of parting with my beloved in Hungary is much more significant proof of the fact that no real change had yet taken place. We had both decided that we'd live together, that we loved each other and that love triumphs if one believes in it. And we really did believe. After the summer camp, she came to Israel and was even accepted for further studies at Tel Aviv University. But her mother, who had vowed never again to set foot in Israel, was horrified. The possibility of her only daughter leaving her to grow old alone broke her heart. The daughter could not see her mother suffer and she broke down, too. We sought a solution. We lived in Budapest for a while and then in Tel Aviv, and together again and apart again.

But in all my talks with her and with her mother, I always declared that "I am not leaving Israel." I enjoyed my stay in Hungary and didn't mind the idea of living there for a while studying or working, as long as it was agreed that we would eventually make our home in Israel and raise our children to speak Hebrew. "This country was not made for people like us to leave," I repeatedly and bluntly told her émigré mother. "I did not spend five years fighting in the army just to throw everything away one year after my discharge and betray all I fought for," I said. And I returned to Israel alone.

CHAPTER 16

Okay. So I spent a month in Central America, and some months in Hungary, then I took the scholastic aptitude tests and decided what I wanted to study. But I still had to do my post-army trip—something special, not the normal South American trek, and certainly not the trendy Far East route that has never appealed to me. That whole new-age scene—yoga, meditation and Buddhism workshops—had always made me cringe. Out of ignorance, for sure, but I felt an arrogant need to be different. Thus I got the idea of doing the 900-kilometer "Cross-Israel Trek," a trip my mother would eventually call my "purification journey."

I packed everything I thought I needed into my sister's post-army India-trip backpack. I decided not to stash water along the way in the Negev Desert, first of all because it was complicated, and secondly because it didn't seem sexy to make such preparations. So instead I carried water for three or four days. If I managed to save my back from the damage of army training, it would never forgive me for what I did to it on this trip.

My cousin was a helicopter pilot at that time, employed to clean high-powered electric cables. So we took off in a chopper at dawn from the center of the country on an amazing low-altitude flight over the expanses of the Negev desert. The helicopter landed near a gas station at the entrance to the city of Beer Sheva and I got off with my heavy gear, just the way I used to on helicopter-transported maneuvers in the army. Then my cousin flew off to go do his job. I got to the main road, and unlike army days, stopped a cab to take me to the university. I turned in my registration forms and continued to Eilat. There I met two friends who had agreed to join me on the first days of my trip.

The next day we climbed the ridge east of the Red Sea, and only then did I realize how heavy my pack was and how unfit I was for such a hike. What the hell was I doing in the middle of the desert with that refrigerator on my back? Why was I tormenting myself like this? Two days later, true to the plan, I took leave of my friends and continued on my own, totally alone. Along the Israel Trail I met solitude in all its levels. I began to write about it while taking shelter inside a small, low-lying cave. Rain was pouring down outside and the ravine began to fill and flocks of mountain goats crossed from one side of the cliff to the other, hopping by the cave entrance and showing me their bellies as I crouched inside — an enchanted, unforgettable moment.

CHAPTER 17

My parents intended to visit me in the town of Mitzpe Ramon. We took a room there for two days and planned to hike together around the western Ramon mountain ridge.

I reached the town before them on our appointed day, and sat on the edge of the canyon waiting for the sun to set — it was a beautiful evening and the sky above turned orange.

I had a regular evening routine throughout my trip. Before nightfall I would cook my supper over a campfire, read or write something with the last rays of light, and when it got totally dark, I would eat in the light of the campfire and, no more than an hour after sundown, I would go to sleep.

On that night, my parents still had not arrived. It began to grow dark and I was getting hungry. I went to the room, left my pack and ventured out to meet civilization. I got some pastries and chocolate milk at the local supermarket, and walked over to the cashier. The people in line gave me strange looks. They moved aside and let me pass them. The cashier cringed with disgust or even fear, giving me an especially dirty look. Suddenly it registered: Without my backpack, after ten days alone in the desert, I must look like a filthy beggar, dusty, sweaty and smelly.

Until that day I had hiked the trail without ever letting go of my backpack, and nearly everyone who saw me traveling this way, alone, gave me an appreciative look and expressed interest in my trip. Some invited me to share a meal on the ground, or even in their nearby home. Everyone treated me nicely, whether in the natural, easygoing manner of wayfarers, or out of simple politeness. As soon as I shed my backpack, however, people's looks changed instantly. I suddenly realized how a beggar or homeless person feels in our society, and it was a shock. I left the supermarket to have a bite nearby but there, too, people moved away and continued staring at me.

Then I went into a grocery shop for some cigarettes and something sweet. Two kids stood in front of the ice-cream cooler, deliberating over what they should get: one expensive chocolate "Magnum" ice cream to share, or two cheap popsicles. I picked up two kinds of chocolate bars and asked the cashier for five packs of Noblesse cigarettes and some mints from the counter behind her. She, too, gave me a suspicious, disgusted look. "Can you afford all of this?" she asked me.

I was stunned. I was so used to playing my usual role in society that I simply could not register the sudden transformation. "Add two Magnums to my bill for those kids," I said. "And may I get anything for you as well?" I asked, and took out my golden credit card.

"Please show me your ID," she answered, and phoned in to clear my card. I smiled politely and waited patiently. I took my little shopping bag and headed back to my hotel room. This time, unlike earlier, I noticed immediately that some of the people walking towards me were moving aside, avoiding eye contact and even getting off the sidewalk. I thought about the difference in appearance between me as a friendly hiker and me as a repulsive outsider: all I had done was take off my backpack.

The evening had turned out strange and slightly unpleasant, but instructive. I had learned something new about myself. Ever since, I've noticed the looks I myself give beggars or homeless people. I have discovered that I, too, like everyone else, regard those "dregs of society" precisely the way our society expects me to.

My parents came out to meet me a second time near the town of Beit Shemesh in the Jerusalem region. The official trail passes by old battle sites and memorials for the heroes of the Burma Road who broke the siege on Jerusalem in 1948. My mother did what she was always wont to do in my childhood: she stopped by every sign and read it aloud for us. Suddenly I hushed her up and said that those damned signs were what made me go to the army and commit crimes in the Occupied Territories.

She was very surprised. I myself am surprised to this very day for what I said on that trail. The words I uttered were in fact chronologically wrong. I had not yet begun to think of my actions in the military as "crimes" at the time, and was certainly not in the habit of using such terminology. On the contrary: I was then still, at least outwardly, convinced that

115

we were enlightened occupiers and that our occupation was a moral one. The link I made in my mind between my military service in the Territories and the war of 1948 was even more astonishing.

But I did say it, and consequently we let the signs go and talked about the War of Independence. No doubt we all agreed back then that it was not easy to judge the generation who fought it, nor could we ever know whether they could have done it any other way. Yet those words that must have emerged from deep inside my subconscious at the time were the reason for my mother later calling my trip a "purification journey." I didn't yet understand what she meant. Now I know it was another milestone in a process that would continue for years.

CHAPTER 18

Traveling alone, one meets people. One day I came across a group of Bedouins, inhabitants of the "unrecognized villages." It was the day after the assassination of Hamas leader Sheikh Yassin and the whole country was rocking. Many text messages were sent to me that day, as I rested at an army pal's home in Arad, a small desert town. The senders suggested, asked, or pleaded with me—depending on their degree of familiarity— not to hike around the Arad Valley and south Hebron hills just then. That particular encounter with the Bedouins got off to a bad start: they thought I had stolen drugs while I was sure they intended to kill me. They followed me in a Subaru pickup truck. They yelled, waved their hands, and called out to me to stop and approach them. I wouldn't stop but rather took the roughest route I could find so their car could not pursue me. Before they got out of the truck I heard them saying, *hada yahudi*— "this is a Jew." There was no doubt in my mind that I was off to meet my maker as revenge for Sheikh Yassin. I stopped, placed the backpack next to me, took out the pistol I had in my top compartment and stuck it under the drawstring of my pants. There were three of them. They moved towards me quickly and were no longer yelling or laughing, but continued to walk in, drifting a bit further apart from each other. Their silent walk seemed very threatening.

I planned my next moves fast. I set my objective and determined my mode of operation accordingly, just as I had done as an officer in the Occupied Territories. If they were armed, I would take at least two of them with me to the hereafter; and if they only had some "cold" weapons on them, I intended to get out of there alive at any cost, even if that meant finishing all three of them. To that end, and judging by the distance separating them, I estimated I'd need about twelve meters so as not to let the third one reach me with a knife. I'd have to draw my pistol by surprise so that if a shoot-out ensued, I'd manage to kill two before the third one opened fire.

As they were about to cross the imaginary line I had drawn in my mind, I looked into the eyes of the oldest of the three, a bearded fellow of about thirty, and yelled *waqef!*—stop! The three halted, surprised. I scanned them quickly. The one on the left, the youngest, moved his coat as if he were about to draw a gun. I drew mine and aimed it at him directly. My pistol was loaded and I meant to open fire, true to plan, one bullet at the fellow on the left, then the older one on the right, and finally the middle one who seemed less threatening. The one on the left had continued to open his coat to reveal the handle of a dagger, but at the sight of my pistol they all stretched their hands out to the sides and froze.

118

I realized that the only weapon they had on them was that dagger. I was instantly reassured and proceeded to plan B. My body felt totally weak and depleted, as after a near collision on the road, or an almost-fall off a cliff. This sensation instantly overcomes you after the passing of some great, concrete fear: one's hands and feet go faint and one's whole body slumps. I looked at the face of the fellow on the right and slowly lowered my pistol to half my height.

That was what a person looked like with a gun pointed at his face. I should know, I've seen plenty. But I have never had a gun pointed at my face before and have no idea what my face would look like. I do know very well what mortal danger feels like, but not this immediate, not with a barrel of a gun aimed at me.

I continued lowering my pistol. The frozen silence that had fallen when I yelled "stop!" remained. I didn't know what I was supposed to do now to get out of that situation, but I acted quickly and without thinking: I put my pistol back in my pants and with my hands held out I proceeded towards the older, bearded man. When I reached him, I clasped his hands, which were still held out, and kissed his cheeks, right, left and right again. I'd seen Arabs who are friends do when they met, although I'd never done it myself until now. The initial tension lifted a bit. I looked at the man with the dagger and saw his coat closed again.

"I thought you wanted to kill me," I said. "I'm sorry."

The expression on the face of the fellow in the middle now changed from fearful to offended. He began shouting: "Who do you think you are? I can send you to join the army up there, they have such a big weapon," he said, and stretched his hands apart like a little child describing something very large. He continued shouting, disconnectedly. "We came to help you, and who are you, and what do you think, and what's a tourist doing with a gun on him, son of a bitch, who are you anyway, who are you anyway . . ." He kept yelling for a long time, and when he fell silent, I answered him, nearly whispering: "When you called me over, I heard *hada yahudi* and thought you had decided to finish me off."

"We thought you were a crazy tourist who didn't understand where he was headed. You were walking in the direction of Dahariya refugee camp and the Palestinians would kill you out there, you idiot."

I apologized some more and signaled to them that I was on my way.

"Don't go there," said the older man. "It's a dangerous area."

"I know where I am and I know where I'm going," I answered. I was on my way north on the marked trail, headed towards kibbutz Amasa. At Tel Arad I had met a nice fellow who suggested I come over and sleep in their community hall. He thought it would be unpleasant to sleep outdoors in those parts. That's where I was headed. I loaded my pack on my back and began walking. I climbed the hill another several dozen meters but felt my legs fail and couldn't go on. The aftershock was acute and nearly paralyzed me.

I climbed another few steps, stopped on a rock at the top of the hill, lit myself a cigarette and tried to calm down. Below I saw the three Bedouins back at their vehicle. They were having difficulty moving it. While chasing me they had left the road and driven among rocks until the pickup got stuck. It also got rather banged up. I took the gun out of my belt and returned it to its secret place inside my pack, then walked down towards them. I offered to help push. They accepted, as they were really in need of assistance. We got the car going and brought it back to the dirt track.

I felt uncomfortable and didn't want to take leave this way. So I asked whether they would join me for coffee. They looked at each other, and then the "middle fellow" answered that a Bedouin may not refuse a cup of coffee, certainly not when offered by an enemy. So they accepted, but not here. They needed to drive up the hill another few hundred meters north, and they said I could join them. It was my direction anyway. The road was so difficult and the ride so slow that if I felt in danger again, I could easily jump out of the truck and escape. I climbed into the open back of the pickup and we drove north.

On the way, the older bearded man gave me his ID. "Here," he said. "Call your dad and tell him you're a guest at this guy's place. Give him all my information, so if anything happens the police will come to me. No problem." I declined, saying I trusted him. He stuck his ID into my pant pocket and said, "Keep it until we part and give the information to anyone. I want you to feel safe."

When we got to a small clump of pine trees they stopped and got out, and so did I.

I began to make coffee while they took out some vodka. They had wandered away from their village because they wanted to have a drink. The "middle fellow"—or "The Explainer" as I came to think of him—appeared to have taken on the job of teaching me about Negev Bedouin culture. He resumed his explanation: "Smoking grass is no problem but alcohol is forbidden in Islam. If I drink and my neighbors see me, it's a disgrace to the whole family. If we want to drink we go far enough so no one from our village will see us."

He explained to me where they lived. I knew this area from my treks in basic training and my later army navigations. When I went alone or with a partner on night navigation exercises, we always peered into those tin shacks. We envied them for drinking coffee or watching television by generator while we had to sweat it out. We cursed them for the occasional new vehicles that were parked outside, which didn't look like they had been bought with the pittance they earned from the measly wheat that grew around their shacks, or from the sheep herded by their young daughters. We were afraid of them, and even more afraid of their dogs.

When we held maneuvers there in the daytime, we traded with them, exchanging canned bully beef from our rations for fresh flatbread. We'd yell "*luf-bita*" among the tin shacks and pens, like some junk monger announcing his wares, and bare-foot children would stream out towards our Hummers, their hands full of fresh bread. They would return to the shacks with two or three tins of meat, which most of us soldiers regarded as dog food anyway. Sometimes, our maneuver orders included an additional objective, either insinuated or outright: "Maintaining our sovereignty in the Negev areas."

We had coffee and they drank some vodka, too. "The Beard"—the one I had kissed on the cheeks—asked me, "Where are you headed here like this?"

I told him about the trip I was on from Eilat to Mount Hermon and that at the moment I was making my way to Amasa.

"Crazy, this fellow" he said to his two mates, and turned back to me, adding, "It's getting late. You won't make it there before nightfall."

He was right. Before I ran into them I had lingered a long time in a failed attempt to photograph a fox that passed me very closely and hid among the rocks. After that failure I treated myself to some "comfort coffee" and a chocolate bar, which I had saved from that morning, and I smoked a few cigarettes. Then they came along, and helping them get their truck unstuck had been time-consuming. Now we had spent nearly an hour in this clump of trees.

"Why did you really try to stop me?" I asked, after deliberating for a long time over whether I should mention the strained circumstances of our first encounter. They looked at each other and were silent for a long time.

"We thought you stole something from us," said The Beard, and fell silent.

"You said you thought I was a crazy tourist," I replied. "Why would a crazy tourist steal anything from you?"

Another long silence fell and I was regretting having raised the matter again. But apparently the alcohol had done its job, for after several attempts on my part to break the silence, and some words in Arabic exchanged among them, The Beard lit up a joint and said, "Look, our herds are down there in the area where you first saw us, and that's where we hide our goods. A few days ago some kilos were stolen from one of our caches," he said, and pointed to the grass he was smoking, making sure I understood.

The Explainer took out another two joints and offered me one.

"I don't smoke," I said.

"Never?"

"Never." And I added, "Just Noblesse cigarettes."

The Beard went on to say that I had passed very close to a large cache and lingered there for a while. "The shepherd down the hill called and said there was a thief hanging out there, snooping around."

I realized that was the place I had tried to photograph the fox.

"But you said *hada yahudi* before you got out of the pickup," I insisted.

"When we walked on and saw your blond hair, we thought you were a girl and began to yell for the fun of it. When we got closer we thought you were a tourist who had no idea where he was going. We yelled at you 'come here!' and you yelled back 'come here yourselves!' From the way you spoke we understood you were a Jew. We got out of the truck to see what you were doing here. That's it. Now you have all my information in your pocket and you know where our stuff is hidden. What more do you need to trust us?"

"Nothing," I said. "I believe you." And I really did. The whole time "The Dagger" sat there, wordless. His Hebrew wasn't very good and it seemed to me that he hadn't quite managed to relax after having my pistol aimed in his face. This friendly sitting around with me seemed not quite to his liking. I was still a bit wary of him myself, and remembered the dagger tucked away inside his coat. When he sat, I could see the curved handle protrude from his trouser belt. I smiled at him and didn't really know what to say to lift the tension. Now it had really gotten very late and I began to pack up my coffee kit and get ready to leave.

"You won't make it before nightfall," repeated The Beard. "Come on over for supper. Keep my ID. Or if you're uncomfortable with that, we can just give you a ride to the main road and you can travel on from there."

It was a hard decision to make. In hindsight, I don't think I would make the same decision—the same mistake—if I had the chance again. On the one hand, I had many reasons to fear these men, and can't say my fears had been totally dismissed. On the other hand, I really did not want to walk around that area in the dark, especially not after what I had been through in the previous few hours. I was also very curious to see up close how these Bedouins lived out there. I wanted to sit inside one of their tin shacks for once, the kind we'd peeked into during our night navigations. I thought of Itamar, my cousin and closest friend in those days, whom I always considered a symbol of levity, unlike me and my heavy-headedness. I wondered what he would do.

"Thanks," I said. "Okay, I'm in."

The Explainer, paragon of Bedouin advocacy, said, "From this moment on, you are a guest. And for the Bedouin, a guest is his honor. Like a family member. No one will hurt you — that would be like spilling our own blood and we would have to avenge you."

His calming words stressed me out even more, but now I was already sitting in the pickup truck and there was no going back. In my head I began to blame Itamar for forcing me to make such a decision and risk my life — what a stupid idea: to blame someone for advice he never even gave! On our way, we passed by a permanent Bedouin settlement. The Beard pointed at it and said, "Those are the biggest shits. Do you know who lives there?"

"Bedouins who agreed to leave their own lands and move to a permanent settlement," I answered confidently. I thought that was the reason they were shits in his mind. He laughed.

"It's a settlement of collaborators from the Occupied Territories," he said. "They live here now after having risked their lives for the Israeli army. So as not to be murdered out there as traitors, they're thrown out here with us. But what goes around comes around, and none of them will ever be safe. They will all be murdered, just like those you settled in Beer Sheva." I noticed especially the way he used the second person plural.

"I never settled anyone there," I said. "I wasn't even aware of this."

He understood and apologized. "You understood what I said, it's just my Hebrew that came out like that. You're okay and you're my guest and my honor."

We went down towards the main road connecting Beer Sheva and Arad. The driver went wild, racing around the dirt track while the two guys in back laughed. He went on that way, and then from the back The Dagger yelled at him in Arabic through the window. The Beard translated for me: the vehicle belonged to The Dagger and he told the driver that if a tire were punctured he'd have to pay for it.

Only then did I remember I was riding in a truck driven by someone both stoned and drunk. Funnily enough—since I had otherwise been obsessed with fear and escape plans—I had overlooked the greatest danger. And I, unlike my light-headed cousin, never got in a car with a driver who'd had more than one beer. I have even been known to leave a party by cab while my pals took the private car in which we'd arrived. And if I was getting a ride somewhere, I would sometimes stop the car and get out in the most godforsaken places if the driver seemed irresponsible.

When we finally reached the road, one tire was already punctured and the spare tire was useless as well. After stopping for consultation and accusations, they decided to continue driving on the rim of the wheel all the way to the village.

At last, we entered a tin pen closed on three sides and sat around a campfire burning in the center. The Explainer continued his anthropological observations. He hid the vodka bottle under some rags in the corner and again explained why drinking was forbidden. Now he also added a warning so I wouldn't forget that I mustn't tell anyone about it. Ridiculous, I thought. After all, the place reeked of the alcohol on their breaths.

Many people joined us and greeted me. The Beard introduced me again and again and always mentioned that I was his personal guest. Ten or more men sat with us. Occasionally young boys and girls would come in and be instantly shooed away. The Explainer informed me that every family has this kind of guest room with a fire burning in the middle. "That's the place for hospitality and every guest is protected by our honor," he said. "That's the nice thing about our life in the desert. You sit here all day quietly, smoking, drinking tea, no problem and no worries. No one can come in here if he's unwanted, not even the police."

There then ensued an argument about the car. The Dagger, in loud Arabic, demanded eighty shekels from The Explainer, forty for each ruined wheel. The Beard translated everything for my sake. I thought that a used wheel and the cheapest tire would never cost less than 120 shekels each. I had a Subaru pickup just like theirs, which would be stolen from me two years later in Beer Sheva, capital of the Negev desert, perhaps by the very same gang or their neighbors. That car would survive six theft attempts, until the one time I forgot to lock the steel chain that connected it to the local power pole every evening.

"It's not a car for Jews," Bedouin drivers used to yell at me through the window. "Sell it to me for 3,000. What, you prefer I take it from you for nothing?"

128

"You can't live in the south with such a jalopy."

"Where do you live? What? You don't answer? Say, isn't that a pity, I'll just follow you all the way."

"It's hard to cross over to Palestinian Dahariya today, a thousand shekels are not worth the risk of stealing it now. Another few weeks and the closure will be lifted, then we'll come pick it up. Too bad, sell it to me now."

I never gave in. I fought and kept it until I lost it honorably to people who have nothing else to do but steal.

The Explainer said he'd give The Dagger two wheels instead of money. He then went off and borrowed a yellow "getaway Subaru" from The Beard and came back half an hour later with the two wheels in his hands and a big smile on his face. "Idiot!" yelled The Beard. "We have enough trouble with them as it is. Why did you steal those wheels, and using my car too!"

"Relax," answered The Explainer. "It's not from them. It's from Jews." He smiled at me.

I smiled back, hiding my amazement at his shamelessness. I added "enjoy!" and they laughed.

Talk around the fire continued in Hebrew the whole time. I felt they were honoring me, for some of them had a hard time expressing themselves. When anyone switched to Arabic, The Explainer or The Beard immediately translated aloud, and after a few phrases the speaker would switch back to Hebrew. Every time anyone older came in, they all got up, and so did I. They greeted him, some with kisses and others with a mere handshake, waited for him to be seated and then sat back in the circle that kept growing towards mealtime.

Children came in bearing large platters of food—beans and rice, vegetables and a pile of thin flatbread. The food was served in large common trays and everyone dipped bits of bread in them, gathering the morsels. I enjoyed the food and The Explainer described each tray as if I were a customer in some gourmet ethnic restaurant. In the middle of the meal, an older man entered and The Dagger got up to greet him. I got up, too, out of habit, but The Explainer, who sat next to me, gripped my shoulder and forced me down again. "No one rises over food. Food comes from God and it is respected more than anyone entering the room." I accepted this new code willingly but pointed to The Dagger. "That's his father," clarified The Explainer. "A man comes from his father. The only thing more important than your father is God himself. You always rise when your father enters."

I continued eating and enjoying the anthropology, until finally the children returned to collect the trays with the leftovers. "This is for the children and women," said The Explainer, pointing at the trays that now contained not much more than some potatoes and bits of bread. Now I was embarrassed and sorry I had eaten so much. What a bunch of hogs, I thought crossly.

After the meal nearly everyone present lit himself a large joint. The Beard called me aside. Then I understood their real reason for inviting me, or at least one of the reasons.

"Look," said The Beard. "You seem a nice kid, blond and Jewish, no one would search you. I could give you three kilos free, then you could sell them in Tel Aviv for 10,000, even

15,000 shekels, depending on how much you sell it for. Then, come back here, I'll sell you each kilo for 300. You'll divide it up into buds and sell each for fifty. This way in a year or two your life will be all set."

I was terribly scared, but didn't want to refuse right away because I feared their reaction. I smiled and kept silent. "Think about it. For you it's nothing." Then he told me how they smuggle the stuff from Egypt. "We have two Jeeps, the kind the Border Patrol uses. We have an army radio with an amplifier and a high antenna. If some traveler gets close, we put on dark shirts and police caps. You can't be arrested for false appearances just because you wore a cap anyone can get in the market.

"We get close to the border around the time the patrol notifies their fellow officers that they're taking a break. We hear the lookout ask the patrol where they are. If they begin to argue over where they are, we know the lookout has identified us and not the patrol, so we go back. If they don't argue, we know we're not being watched. So we approach the border and within five minutes we unload the stuff from four camels and put it in our Jeeps.

"Sometimes we press our radio apparatus and then the lookout and the patrol can't talk to each other. They switch to an alternate frequency and we switch there too. They have no chance of catching us. We also have our people inside in case the army or police lays an ambush. You have nothing to worry about. You get everything here from me, where we met earlier. Come on your hikes and we'll meet. Think about it. For you it's nothing."

A young man arrived at the shack and sat down. Hot tea was served out of a pot that had been standing over the burning coals all the while. I returned to the circle after talking with The Beard. Some of the men had already gone and the rest continued to converse quietly, in Hebrew again, about very little.

Suddenly, voices went shrill and Arabic was spoken. Shouts were exchanged between the young man who entered and The Dagger who, until now, had sat quietly the whole time. They both rose to their feet at once and The Dagger drew his knife with a sudden movement. I was petrified. The Beard got up and yelled in Hebrew at The Dagger: "Sit down! You will not spill blood in my home nor in front of my guest!" He then turned to the new guy who joined us and yelled at him: "Do not offend my honor and don't make the conflict worse. You did not have to come here and speak. Go away!"

I was stunned. A moment earlier, an easy conversation was being held over tea. Then in an instant tempers flared and a dagger was drawn with obvious lethal intent. Everyone sat back down quietly. When talk resumed, The Explainer interpreted for me: "The family of the guy who came in and his family" — he pointed to The Dagger — "have had a blood feud for a long time now. The present situation is that his family" — the Dagger's — "killed one less, because the last time the whole matter was supposed to be closed, two people were killed by mistake rather than one. Now one of them must die. The guy who came in, it's alright that he's here, but he shouldn't have spoken about the feud. As soon as he did, The Dagger was obliged to take revenge on that one."

Then The Explainer pointed to The Beard and added: "He's right, it should not be in this house, and not in front of you. That's too dangerous. You might talk."

I realized I had to get away. Outside, night had fallen and I had no idea what to do. I was afraid of The Dagger and of that whole violent scene. I was afraid of the smuggling offers I had received. I was a good kid, an officer fresh out of the army. I simply could not fathom where I found myself. The gathering grew smaller. Everyone smoked endless quantities of grass, each person rolling his own huge joint. I kept chain-smoking my own Noblesse cigarettes like crazy and drinking a lot of tea, trying to think of a way out.

As far as these guys were concerned, obviously I had accepted their invitation to sleep over. But I felt I had gone a step or two too far. My three acquaintances left and said they'd be back shortly. I stayed there alone with a tall, thin fellow who seemed very gentle and non-threatening. I began to calm down. He introduced himself as the older brother of The Explainer and asked whether I wanted coffee. He placed a pan on the fire and roasted the coffee beans, then put the beans in a mortar and began to grind. He passed me the copper mortar and pestle and suggested I grind some myself. He, too, like his younger brother, explained things: "It's a great honor for a guest to grind coffee at the invitation of his hosts."

It reminded me of a trip I'd taken in sixth grade to the Shibli village, the Bedouin encampment for tourists in the north of the country. With his quiet, even sickly voice, he named a few people and asked me whether I knew them. "No," I answered.

"They're very famous," he said. "Heads of clans from Ramle and Lod." He had made their personal acquaintance in jail.

Again I tensed up.

"I was inside for three years for a cocaine deal I made here." Why the hell was he telling me this?

"An undercover agent, son of a bitch from Beer Sheva, caught me red-handed and had recordings. We could have finished him off before the trial but my lawyer cut me a good deal—a three-year sentence is nothing for the quantity I had. Cocaine is not what my brother does, it's serious. Ultraorthodox Jews from Jerusalem in Mercedes cars and special cabs from Tel Aviv came to us. It was good money until that son of a bitch had me. I just got out a month ago, still on two years' probation, but the son of a bitch will pay. We'll screw him. I'm just sitting tight until my suspended sentence is over. But I know where he lives, I know where his wife works and I keep my eye on him constantly. Coffee is ready. *Tfadal* (please, help yourself)."

"*Shukran* (Thanks)."

We drank coffee. A few minutes passed and then The Dagger came in and joined us at the fire, his head very close to mine. The other two came in as well, and judging from their smell and their conduct, they had been drinking again.

"Are you planning to sleep here?" asked The Dagger in a near-whisper.

"I've been invited to. Why not?" I answered, concealing my fervent wish to get away.

"No good, you sleeping here," he whispered.

"Why?" I asked.

The two brothers and The Beard came closer and sat next to us, so The Dagger fell silent. The conversation among the other men resumed. Then The Dagger used another moment he had with me alone and continued whispering: "Your pistol is worth more than your life. It's a clean weapon, without a record. And it also offended our honor. Not good, you sleeping here."

Then unexpectedly, my luck turned. They had run out of vodka and wanted more. The Explainer asked his big brother for money, but he refused. He pleaded, began to sound nervous and occasionally burst into silly drunken laughter. He held out hugging hands to me and to The Beard, who was very drunk as well.

"Where do you want to buy it?" I asked.

"In Arad," he answered. I realized this was an opportunity. "I have no money on me," I lied. "But if you take me to Arad I will get you two bottles with my credit card. It's on me. I owe you a lot more."

After the money issue was settled, he began to look for a car he could borrow. He called various people on his cell phone and asked for one. After several refusals, his cell phone minutes ran out. I handed him my cell phone and he continued trying.

"Why can't we just go in the pickup?"

"It's stolen. We don't ride stolen cars on the road to Arad."

After much pleading The Beard agreed to let us all ride in his yellow Subaru, after The Explainer promised to pay the fine if we got caught.

135

"It's a clean car, mine," explained The Beard. "But no annual vehicle inspection and no insurance." I picked up my pack and followed them. The Beard turned to me and said, "Leave it here, no one will touch it." That sounded ludicrous to me after all that crime lore I'd just listened to, and I had no intention of coming back with them anyway. "Look, this is my home," I said. "I haven't let go of it once in my whole trip. Even if my own father came to watch over it, I wouldn't leave it here."

He was convinced. We drove off. For the second time in a day — and in my entire life — I was sitting in a car driven by a stoned drunk. His ID was still in my pocket. We stopped at the town entrance and walked to the nearest store. Again I took my pack, and the same argument resumed.

"And what if your car were stolen? You've got to understand, it's my home."

The Beard gave up. I bought the two bottles of vodka and we left the store. Before we were out of earshot of the shopkeeper, and not far from a group of boys sitting on the sidewalk, I took The Beard's ID out of my pocket and said I was staying in Arad, sleeping over at a friend's house. "Thanks for everything, your hospitality and the meal."

"Why all of a sudden like this? Come on, stay with us." They pressured me. I wouldn't give in. The Beard tried once more: "Call your friend. If it's okay, we'll take you there. If not, come stay with us." Then I used the magic word that over the past few hours I'd learned worked in favor of whoever drew it first: "It's my honor you're testing," I said assertively. "I've made up my mind and I'm going. I'll come back to discuss your offer with you later," I said, adding another lie to this surreal day's assortment. As soon as I uttered the word "honor," and perhaps because I promised to come back, the two relented. The Beard took his ID and off they drove.

My friend wasn't home, the youth hostel in town was closed, and another hotel turned out to be a brothel. I slept on the lawn of a soccer field and woke up at 4:30 a.m. from the automatic sprinklers. I cursed my Creator and all of his creations, then waited at Arad's filthy commercial center for the first bus. Only yesterday I had hung around there feeling like a prince, telling anyone ready to listen that I had hiked all the way there from Eilat.

"You're really obsessed, eh?" was a typical flattering response. What a nice place this was two days ago. Now it looked like a pile of stinking filth. I took the first bus to Shoqet Junction, skipping the section of my trail from Tel Arad to Amasa, and continued my beautiful trek northbound.

Perhaps I had been to a tin shack of particular circumstances, I don't know. But inside that shack I met an altogether different segment of our society, one that, for the likes of me, does not really exist. When they appear for a moment in our lives, we mainly feel a certain anger at their very existence. The question that really bothers us is how to be rid of them, not how to improve their lot.

The next day I began to think about them. At first I thought about that undercover policeman who might really get hurt, and then about the poor fellow who got up in the morning to a car without wheels. But later, my thoughts went deeper, into things I had not actually seen but now knew existed.

I began to ask myself questions I had never asked before: Where is the State's responsibility to a woman who is raped in a locality where the police dare not enter? Where will a Negev Bedouin shepherd live once he decides to become a law-abiding citizen? How will he make a living? Who profits hugely from the situation as it presently exists? Who am I to expect the Bedouins to abide by the law? What would I do in their position? And who am I to preach to them about women's rights? And what will actually become of the collaborators' families? Will they be integrated into the misery and general helplessness of their new community, or will they go on being excluded and marked for death even there? And the children? What chance do those boys and girls who served me food inside that tin shack have to escape the hopeless, vicious circle into which they were born?

CHAPTER 19

From Shoqet Junction I headed north towards the trail that follows the "green line" to the foothills of Mount Sansana, and from there I followed the orange-blue-white markings along the winding way amid pine groves and tended wheat fields. I was bound for Kibbutz Lahav. On the rolling hills, I saw an interesting purple plant that carpeted the ground near the trail. I'd never seen the plant before. I strayed off the trail towards the colorful stain of impressive purple thorns. Another hill rolled on from there in fresh green splendor and almond trees. I kept veering away from the trail, and as I approached the almond grove I noticed a small flock of goats, and eventually a goatherd who approached me and waved his hands towards the dirt track, as if to show me that I was lost. In fact, he wanted to get me off his land.

"*Salaam 'aleik,*" I said. "My name is *Naim.*"

He returned my greeting but kept pointing to the road below, saying "*hai tarikak*"—"There's your road."

I tried to explain that I was only taking a closer look at the plants and that I would soon be off, and that I meant well.

I don't know how much he understood from all of this, but it was obvious that I came in peace. I hid my pistol as soon as I noticed him so as not to scare him. Sitting down under one of the trees, I invited him to join me for a bit. He did not sit down but kept running back and forth, picking up an occasional stone and throwing it at one of the goats who insisted on nibbling on an almond tree instead of eating the fresh grass. I took out a campers' gas stove and coffee pot, even though I had drunk some only a little earlier, and asked, "What will you have, tea or coffee?" He waved off my invitation and continued to pace around. "Tea or coffee?" I insisted.

"Tea," he said.

I gestured again for him to take a seat on the rock I'd left vacant, then I sat on the ground beside him and prepared "tea" — an infusion of sage, mint and two or three thyme sprigs for their bitter flavor. This was one of the tips I'd gotten from some tank-crew members who had served with us on the northern border. I liked the combined flavor and hoped my guest-host, too, would take to it. I handed him a glass. He was impressed with how fast water boiled on my brand new camper gas coil-stove.

There had been days when I sent my subordinates to look for explosive charges along the fence that surrounds the industrial plant in the Etzyon settlement block where these very stoves are produced. *Oh, Tuviah, dear Tuviah, my childhood hero, if you only knew what we do to the Arabs of Gush Etzyon, the area you failed to reach with the medication and food you had carried on your back. If you only knew that my superiors* named the Palestinian village of Nakhlin *"a malignant tumor in the heart of the Etzyon Jewish settlement block"! And we drew our conclusions accordingly: they should be treated as cancer. But no one would back us up when it became known that we had humiliated or harassed them, for that was not what we had been ordered to do—saying "we just said cancer." If you really were that good-hearted boy I've always envisioned, you would certainly be glad not to have arrived there now, and that with your death you granted nineteen more years of relative freedom to those unhappy villages.*

"*Qadesh 'umri?*"—"How old do you think I am?"—asked the goatherd. I looked at him, thought he must be fifty-something, but didn't want to offend him. I wanted him to win his game. So just to play it safe, I said forty-eight years old— unintentionally, I had blurted out a number that was highly charged in this particular landscape (resonating, naturally, with the 1948 war). He chuckled. For a moment I wasn't sure whether I should raise or lower it, but he asked again, and now, no longer knowing what to say, I answered truthfully: "I assume you're fifty-five." He went on chuckling and reached into his shirt pocket, taking out an ID—the orange-colored ID of a Palestinian.

Had he known how he made me feel as he reached for his orange ID and handed it to me, he certainly wouldn't have done it. From my pastoral hike in nature, on which I had gone to seek interesting sights and people and to photograph unfamiliar plants, and to enjoy an occasional cup of tea or coffee, he threw me right back to Qalandiya Checkpoint, to Beitar

Checkpoint, to our "forceful shows of presence" in villages and towns, to the violent curfews, arrests, suspect detentions and humiliation of passers-by. What a fatal gesture this was: unbuttoning the gray shirt pocket, looking downwards and half-right to the pocket, leafing through pieces of paper and his wallet, and holding out the ID.

I shuddered, surprised, and didn't understand why such a shudder attacked my body all of a sudden. I tried to keep a calm face, not to spoil the friendly atmosphere that had already taken hold of us. "Look how old I am," he said. *Year of birth: 1931*, I read. "Yes, I am seventy-three years old, and I remember '48 and '67 very well. Anyone living close to the earth," he continued, "in peace and quiet with everyone, lives a long life and stays strong."

And I thought, seventy-three years old and this fellow was still throwing stones at his goats and running around here like a demon out of hell—no doubt his theory serves him well. We sipped on, and after some moments of silence he began to tell me his story, or more precisely the story of the place where we were sitting. His Hebrew was not good, and my Arabic consisted of no more than a few remnants of the "occupation-ese" I had spoken until only a year earlier.

He spoke slowly and I stopped him every time I didn't understand. We often switched to pantomime. He was such a cute grandpa. "See that row of boulders, down there, and the ditch?" he said.

"I see it."

"Do you know what that is?"

142

On one side of the boulders lay a dirt track, immediately followed by a vast, carefully tended wheat field, undoubtedly belonging to the nearby kibbutz. On the other side, where we were sitting, was a kind of meadow with that purple carpet that lured me there to begin with, and the almond grove that seemed to be growing wild and untended amidst white limestone surfaces, small un-irrigated trees without a sign of modern farming—in sharp contrast to the green field below us. "These stones are the 1967 border."

I was not surprised, knowing that the marked trail passed along the "green line" in this region, and I thought he was going back to his waving mode that he first used to signal to me that I'd lost my way. But he wasn't.

"These boulders were rolled down by me and my father in 1948. Until then we had inhabited that hill over there," he said, pointing west. He described his home and his family and neighbors there. I didn't always manage to follow what he was saying but I did understand that he was naming the large families and counting the sheep and goat flocks and describing houses and streets.

Then he told me how one day soldiers came and ordered everyone to leave. The soldiers fired in the air and announced that whoever did not leave would be killed. He described their flight on carts, on foot, with their livestock and all the belongings they could carry. All the rest was left behind. He said people went east towards the main road, to the hill route winding from Beer Sheva to the South Hebron Hills, and from there to Hebron, and further north to Jerusalem, Ramallah,

Nablus, Jenin and still further north to Nazareth. Some turned north to Jenin and are living in refugee camps to this very day. Others continued eastward to the Kingdom of Jordan. Heads of families demanded that all villagers stick together, but they argued among themselves over where they should turn and could not agree, so they parted ways. His father—whose name I do not recall, although he said it many times and even showed it to me in his ID—would not continue.

"He said he was climbing this hill," said the goatherd, pointing north-east to the ruins of the hamlet above us, "and stayed there because he wanted to keep his land in sight." Everyone, even his wife and son, tried to persuade him to walk on because the soldiers would arrive soon to expel them from there, too. "My father said that if they come, we shall move on to the next hill, from where we can see this hill from where we can see our land."

First they slept there in the open, and during their first night they saw the soldiers settling into their home. Then they began to put up small pens for their livestock, and when they realized the soldiers were not coming to chase them away, they slowly settled into their new dwelling, refugees just a few kilometers from their home. With time they began to mark the borders of their new domain—they marked the western limit with these boulders that they rolled downhill.

When a ceasefire was declared, their private border was marked in the maps as the international border between Israel and the Hashemite Kingdom of Jordan. Thus they could remain on their newly settled land. They tended their flocks, planted these almond trees, and lived off this rocky patch that is so much less fertile than the land below, but they were blessed by God and managed, surviving hard times. So it was until 1967—"when your army came once again."

This time they were not expelled, but "since then, to this day, every day is worse, and the past few years, since you brought us Arafat, have been especially bad." Soldiers come and seal their water cisterns, settlers steal their goats, and most of the sons leave and go north to the towns in search of work, where it is even worse. But he was staying here. Here he would die, he said, and gazed at his father's land.

He spoke, too, of King Hussein, who betrayed him personally. "I am Bedouin, and loyal to the king, and so was my father to his dying day. In 1948, Abdallah, the king's grandfather, couldn't get us back our lands. In 1967, there was a big war and even strong Egypt lost. The king had no choice, but we remained and waited for him to come save us from you. We knew he was weaker so we waited, faithfully. The king betrayed us when he declared that these lands were not his, that they belong to the Palestinians, to Arafat and his mafia, damn them." He cursed the leaders of the Palestinian Authority with every abomination he knew in Arabic and Hebrew and Occupation-ese, a rich language when it comes to cursing. He said he was still loyal to the king but angry at him, very angry.

Obviously, for this seventy-three-year-old, nothing would be resolved in his lifetime, and I was sorry for him. He had touched me, this grandpa-goatherd. He not only touched me but cast a thin, primal and very personal ray of light into a dark

145

area in my own consciousness. This light would grow stronger and bring with it a new truth, or perhaps, in fact, merely a new awareness of an old truth. And perhaps it would also be true to say that he extinguished something inside me.

CHAPTER 20

Further along my trek, in the Jerusalem hills, I deviated once more from the official trail and looked for the ruins not marked on the map. The pine woods planted by the pioneers and their successors in order to make a just claim to their land, our land, now told me their additional story, a story of a land that had been lost. Stone terraces, which must have been cultivated continuously from the days of King David of old until the late Arab Period, are crumbling here under the dense roots of pine trees. Whole villages and lives are still hidden here.

I walked around the ruins of Beit Tul village above Abu Ghosh, and imagined it back to life. I walked the alleys of my imagination amidst the remnants of homes, stepped on muddy ground thick with dung, and saw sheep and goats being led by herders into their pens, fenced in by the *sabar*—prickly pear— thorns, many of which can still be seen on the ground, alive and continuing to transform sunlight into sugar in the wondrous way of all plants. Here also was a large cave that served as shelter for work- and pack animals.

And down here an advanced terrace system had been developed, and irrigation ditches were dug for swamping. Over there a low-lying structure stored crops, and here, next to the vineyard, the guard used to sleep all through the grape-picking season. The vine branches had not yet surrendered and were persisting in their losing fight against the Israeli forestation projects. Here was the well around which women used to sit with their jars, gossiping and sharing their day-to-day news, their husbands' deeds and sons' capers. Here, just as on the bench at the exit of the grocery shop in my own village, all the juicy local news was gleaned—bitter, sad and delightful. And here was the water cistern. I could imagine the faces of farmers during a dry winter, worried at the sight of the cistern not yet full. I wondered how the villagers shared the water and the land, and what kind of leadership was the custom.

I had a similar experience at En Hindak, another water spring along the trail. It is a popular picnic site in which countless Israeli hikers walk the candle-lit tunnel, bathe in its cold water, and eat watermelons cooled in the spring water. Now I came out of the shallow tunnel along one of the ditches, which had dried up. From one plot of land to another, from one terrace down to the next, I followed the imaginary irrigation track all the way to the large dam above which a huge fertile silt fan had formed.

Facing the dam, which was reminiscent of the Wailing Wall with its large square stones, I stood and admired this great project, probably built jointly by many farmers. Then I climbed back over the dam and chose another aqueduct, following it in the opposite direction this time, back to the spring. Here again were fertile plots with low-lying stone fences, more systems of irrigation ditches and man-made rocky stairs ascending from one plot to the next, all fighting a losing battle against the pine roots. The upper terraces, adjacent to Even Sapir *moshav*, have been tractor-plowed and contained no traces of the previous irrigation system.

I wondered where those people were, those who had once cleared all the stones and built this whole farming system. I wondered how I was so familiar with all these things — Canaan-ite Tel Arad, with the palace of King Ahab in Jezre'el, the Roman antiquities of Beit She'an and Jerusalem, the Roman roads and milestones, the ancient Limes forts along the south-ern border of the Roman Empire in the Negev, the series of hideouts built along the Judean plain and in the Galilee that served the Jewish rebels; how was I so familiar with Tel Megiddo and the Armageddon tale, the Crusader forts of Belvoir and Montfort and Qal'at Namrud and — skipping the Helenists and their legacy in Jerusalem — the bridges and railways and train stations of the Ottoman Empire days, and the police stations and forts remaining from the British Mandate. How could I have trekked this country far and wide without acquainting myself with the most prominent archeological stratum, right here in front of my very eyes?

Later, in the years following my long hike, I worked as a tour guide in this very area, leading family trips and immigrant youth groups. As I hiked on my preparatory rounds, the official signs came alive, placed there for history and posterity by the

149

national parks authority and nature reserve administration, innocent explanatory texts or signposts directing one's thinking towards the one and only truth.

I began to re-read them, and the girl who stole my Holocaust forced me to fill in the images with new faces, truths and facts. I faced the plaque describing the valorous battles around Kibbutz Tzova, one among hundreds of such plaques throughout the country perpetuating the memory of dead Jewish underground fighters. The tin plaque itself now contained stories that my eyes could read, like those stories I never told my interviewers before going to Miami: victories now contained the vanquished, the enemy was now also embodied in the plaques — its fighters, women, children, homes, herds and lifestyle.

In the Jerusalem hills I also made up my first fables. During the following years, as I earned my living leading tours, I would make up and refine and tell many more fables, stories and legends about plants, animals, geographic areas and historical epochs. But this particular one I never shared with my travelers. It was one gradually honed as the feelings it represented grew deeper and my knowledge of botany grew broader — but I kept it secret forever.

The Pine Tree Fable

For the past millennia, only a few pine trees grew in the Jerusalem hills, their provenance unknown. But the pine trees commonly seen in the Jewish National Fund — planted woods were imported from Europe. This species is foreign and altogether different from the local vegetation, which has undergone a long process of integration into its environment during millions of years of evolution.

The oak, pistacio, buckthorn and hawthorn—indigenous Mediterranean trees and bushes—live side by side in a competitive interrelationship, as in every society, each fighting for its own place but also living in harmony with its surroundings and neighbors. Sarsaparilla, honeysuckle, prickly asparagus and many other creepers and bushes grow around them. In springtime, the open space they leave around their own bit of ground is filled with numerous seasonal wild flowers, the best known of which are cyclamens, anemones, narcissi, irises and local orchids. With the winter rains, seeds of therophytes sprout and cover the floor of Mediterranean woods like a lush, green carpet.

Not so the pine. It does not allow the local vegetation to live in its midst. The pine's needles secrete toxins that prevent the sprouting of bush and flower seeds. The needles' bitter, toxic resin prevents cattle and sheep from eating them. Eventually, when the needles fall off, they create a thick suffocating layer on the ground, preventing any new seeds from sprouting and joining the living habitat around the pine.

The scientific name for when a plant suppresses the growth of another in its proximity is "allelopathy." Pine roots are strong and crack the local bedrock, eventually turning it to dust. They do the same to the foundations of man-made structures as well.

However, the pine tree burns easily because of the flammable resin flowing in its veins. When ignited, it burns and disappears just as fast as it took over its new territory.

But the pine has one more unique trait: right after the fire, its seeds sprout in huge quantities. The fire destroys the woods and everything in it. Numerous other seeds that have so far been locked under the toxic needles lose their vitality in the heat and die. Not so the pine seeds, which are disseminated in two kinds. The first kind, which we shall name "simple," is ejected from the pine cone and will sprout easily with the first rain. The other, which we shall name "long-standing," is locked in the pine cone for years, waiting until a disaster wakes it from its long hibernation. In a forest fire, the intense heat opens up the cone and revives the seed, bringing it back to life.

This wondrous biological feature enables our friend the pine to come alive out of the flames and reconstruct its home and territory, whose gates are closed to all others.

CHAPTER 21

One of my favorite sites in Israel is a spring called 'En Yizre'el. It is located about half an hour's walk from my parents' home. I used to go there as a child without asking for permission, for I knew I would not be allowed to cross the main road connecting Afula and Beit She'an by myself. It was an enchanted spot—a pool of clear water hidden inside a thick eucalyptus clump surrounded by wild cane and reeds. Hidden paths led through the tall reeds to the bank.

In my youth, my father tended plots of land close to the spring and we grew melons and watermelons as well as a field of sunflowers. I got to work there during my summer vacations. Lunch break on a hot summer day among the trees around the pool, bathing in the nude while a melon or watermelon cooled in the chilly water—it was pure delight. Dipping my face in the cold water never failed to inspire me with optimism and joy.

Among the eucalyptus trees around the pool stands a memorial for the late Tzvi Karmeli, who fell in the battle of Zar'in. His name was hewn into a basalt memorial, but he too—or so I felt as a child—was connected to me just like

Tuvya Kushnir, almost like family. His name was also intoned at our commemoration ceremonies, when Gideon Yavin, one of the *moshav*'s veterans, with a voice deep and strong, used to read out the names of the fallen heroes of my *moshav*. Furthermore, my parents purchased the Karmeli farm in Kfar Yehezkel, and a year later I was born there. When we children would reach the spring as a group—on horseback, or during a youth movement or school outing—I would boast of my personal link to Tzvi Karmeli, commemorated in those woods around the spring.

But what was that battle over Zar'in? I never asked this question, neither as a child nor as a teenager. I knew that Zar'in was the village situated there before Kibbutz Yizre'el was founded. But where did that village disappear to? Where did all the people and animals go? What happened to the fields and fruit groves? I never asked, and was never told. I knew there were archeological findings next to Kibbutz Yizre'el and that after a thorny hedge was burned, one could easily spot broken earthenware and even ancient coins underneath.

Some people claimed that the remnants of King Ahab's winter palace were buried there. So for the Bar Mitzvah of one of my neighbors we prepared a play and performed it at the archeological site above the spring. We staged the story of the king and his wife Jezebel. If I remember correctly, I played the part of the queen. In our show, as in the Bible, wicked Jezebel sent her husband shopping. He had to purchase the plot of land belonging to Navot the Yizre'elite, probably a lovely grove near the Yizre'el spring.

Navot, however, refused and said something like "Sorry, your majesty, but I cannot leave the land of my forefathers. It is not for sale and never will be."

Ahab returned to his palace and wept bitter tears for not having fulfilled the wishes of his wicked wife. "Why are you crying like a child?" asked the queen. Ahab answered that the fellow wasn't selling, so it appeared they would not be able to expand the palace garden this year. Jezebel screamed at her spouse that he was no king, just a miserable wimp, and that she was taking his royal seals from their bedside drawer and going off to solve this little problem herself.

She sent a gang of thugs to stone Navot to death with rocks from our valley. Ahab inherited his land—murdered and inherited, as the holy book says.

Now it was God's turn to send his own thugs, punish the culprits, sort things out. In our play, Elijah came wrapped in a white sheet, just like the Passover play, and furiously yelled at the king, predicting that not a single male offspring of his would survive and that he and his wife and her wickedness would be punished. Ahab's dynasty was indeed severed and his wicked wife was severely punished for the murder and land theft. She did not even have the privilege of proper burial; her hands and skull were found scattered on the soil she so coveted.

Navot's land—Ahab's land.

Zar'in land—Our land.

After the show and the applause, we climbed down the trail from the palace ruins to the spring, ate flatbread with humus and pickles, and rope-glided like Tarzan from a eucalyptus tree down into the cold spring water. It was a great Bar Mitzvah party.

I felt a childish pride about the story of Ahab and Navot's vineyard: here was my father and the rest of the *moshav* farmers tending the land of honest, decent Navot the Yizre'elite! What a wonderful reconnection to our origins and roots deep in this earth—two thousand years after we left, we have returned to the land of our forefathers, to tend Navot's abandoned vineyard.

Today, without my Holocaust, I sometimes try to imagine what happened in Zar'in when Golani infantry battalion 13 entered the village and cleansed its houses of their inhabitants, "because they put up heavy resistance," as the ceremony texts put it. I've heard that Tzvi Karmeli was killed by a mine that he and his mates went out to lay at the spring. A mine at a spring? The spring of a neighboring village? Impossible. I can't believe that.

After all, they burned our fields, they were thieves and murderers, and we defended ourselves and tended the land that we had purchased with money earned by the toil and sweat of our brows. We fought disease, mosquitoes and malaria. We built by day and guarded by night. In the books I read, the *Palmah* commandos carried out their secret missions while carefully avoiding unnecessary harm to civilians. An explosive charge at a village spring? Impossible. Simply impossible.

We tend Navot's vineyard, indeed. But from whom and how have we inherited this land? I don't know if things could have been done differently, and the truth is I don't know what really went on. This is actually the worst fact of all: we know the story about Ahab, who murdered and inherited, we are familiar with Gideon's path down Gilboa Mountain to Harod spring and Sisra's escape route after his army sank in the valley's mud. We are learned, so we even know the geological epochs in which the Gilboa emerged and its strata formed, We know that some of them are water-penetrable and others are not, and thus Artesian springs were formed, like 'En Yizre'el and Harod spring nearby.

We learned all of this in school, and we saw all of it on our youth movement outings. But we don't have an inkling of what happened here yesterday, right here, in our own 'En Yizre'el, the beautiful spring that over the years has also turned into a barbecue site where piles of trash abound after weekends and public holidays. The rushes and reeds that used to grow down to the water are no more. The eucalyptus clump has thinned out and the old pump house in the center of the pool has been cleaned and emptied of its equipment.

The basalt memorial still stands there, commemorating Tzvi Karmeli, but for me it is a reminder of something more, even if only blurred: the memory of the men, women and children who lived in their village, got up in the morning, tended their trees, herded their livestock, pumped water from the spring, built stone houses, prayed to God to grant them a good harvest, loved, hated, married, bore children, were unfaithful, happy, annoyed, cheated, stole, died, buried, cried. Lived. Villagers, owners of property, who became homeless overnight, left their houses and trudged south on the road at the foot of

157

Gilboa Mountain, towards the city of Jenin. I met their children and grandchildren face-to-face in the refugee camps, on behalf of Saul. Not the king. The chief of staff.

I led three organized tours to Yizre'el Hill and the spring, and I always told my guests the sensational biblical tale of the weak king and the wicked queen. I described the palace and the life perpetuated by the mute stones as I envisioned them, and sometimes I added, incidentally, some basic information about "old" Zar'in village, its huge area—nearly 24,000 dunams—or its population, which used to number 1,650. Sometimes, at the lovely lookout over Harod Valley, I included with the names of *moshav* and kibbutz settlements the names of one or two of the villages that used to be there but were no longer.

Naturally, I told them the tale of "land redemption": that was, after all, the point of climbing up to the lookout. I told them the story of Joshua Hankin and his friends who, with Jewish funds, purchased the lands of the valley from the Arab Sursuk family. Along the "secret valley" route down the slopes of Mount Gilboa, I once took the liberty of mentioning the "human tragedy" of the vassals, adding it delicately to the "redemption story." After all, we had bought the lands visible from the lookout for good money, and there was nothing to hide. I mentioned those workers, baking in the heat of this valley before we came to replace them, the people who had tended the fields in return for a small portion of the harvest. The rest of the harvest went to the landowners, who then sold that very same land to us.

These owners, probably through some kind of bribe, obtained their ownership claims from some Turkish official. But who was that official anyway? What right had he to give out ownership claim certificates and say whose land it was? And how was it that we Israelis, with the Turkish ownership certificates in our possession, gave that dubious land-grab such decisive importance, elevating it to a near-sanctified status, whereas in today's narrative — as I have witnessed myself — we disregard those documents and wave the locals off, even while they hand over all kinds of maps and crumpled yellow sheets of paper to some "officer in charge" — such as myself!

Naturally, I didn't share this detail with my tourists. I didn't tell them what I had learned in my military service about those ownership certificates of Ottoman Empire days and the ways of taking possession of land. I only suggested we be somewhat "humane" for a moment and think about the disaster that befell the families of those vassals, who were deprived even of their right to a life of miserable slavery, when we, with our money, "redeemed" the lands of the Jezre'el Valley. Unlike the landowners such as the villagers of Zarin, those poor penniless vassals were mentioned in our geography classes at school, but where did they go? How? How did they survive? Where are they now?

PART THREE

CHAPTER 22

My Holocaust was stolen from me in that village, but I understood nothing yet. Changes taking place in me were of the internal kind and I was unaware of them until my encounter with "Breaking the Silence," as the organization would eventually be known. My activity in this group would gradually peel off the layers and make my new self surface, first into consciousness and then, later, into words and action. This process was slow at first, but after a while I felt I was sliding down a slope, losing grip on my sense of self. I lost more and more components of my previous identity as a new one was being formed, as yet undefined, mostly based on what I no longer believe in.

Nowadays I can no longer draw the kind of value-triangle we used to sketch for ourselves in the youth movement. Back then we sat in a circle around a large sheet of paper on the floor of our meeting house. The counselor drew a big triangle on the paper and, next to each point, wrote a word representing a set of values: "Jewish," "Zionist," "Israeli." Each member in turn would mark a spot inside the triangle and write his or her name closest to the identity they felt most affiliated with.

Finally, everyone would explain why they marked the spot where they did: why they were, in fact, first and foremost a Zionist, and then Israeli and only last a Jew. Why they considered whoever placed their names in the middle hypocrites. Were I to participate in such a game today, my name would probably be found outside the triangle, contrary to the rules.

The phone call from Yehuda Shaul was strange. A common acquaintance had referred him to me, and he called one week before I took off on my Israel Trail trek. My cousin handed me the phone and said that some madman was rattling off some surreal ideas. I was in a state of deep crisis over my breakup with my sweetheart abroad, and in no state of mind for such folly. Still, I agreed to be interviewed by him the night before I set out on my journey.

I had returned defeated from my last visit to Hungary. I didn't have it in me to leave Israel, and she could not possibly leave her own family. For me, leaving my homeland would be a total betrayal of my upbringing as well as a personal betrayal of my father, who had once disowned his favorite cousin for having left the country. I remembered Dad's harsh words that I heard as a child: "He stabbed us in the back by leaving the country," he said to me and my sisters.

When I realized that the battle for my love was lost, I cut off all contact with her: no phone, no mail, no holiday greetings. And every message from her met only this painful reply: "Sadly, I cannot answer you. I am busy healing. Please do not contact me again."

For the first time in my life, not everything was going smoothly or as planned. On my last flight home I suddenly panicked at the prospect of sinking into depression. I had always been a stout fellow and by that time I had grown a hearty paunch. I imagined myself getting as fat as a pig, wallowing in bed every day, not showering, not brushing my teeth, being unemployed and disconnected from my environment. Yet just like an American film about an adolescent girl who no longer finds any sense in her life, I opened an old notebook I had with me. It still contained some bits of technical army service stuff: the amount of fuel needed for APCs on standby, a tally of ammo in the company bunker, the names of men missing at roll call and the list of their excuses, as well as a planned schedule of soldiers' leaves.

I'm a chronic notebook saver and have a particular liking for my old notebooks that contain navigation routes that I was required to commit to memory: every line includes an azimuth in degrees, a meter count for walking in that direction, and a few words describing the route:

120, 450—descent down the range to a curve in the ravine.

360, 500—descent down the ravine to a clump of trees.

I loved those navigations and miss them terribly. No hike compares to them. I leafed through the notebook and recalled the fantastic sensation of power in my body after walking for dozens of kilometers, and the desert or hilly landscape described by those few figures and words. I usually navigated exceptionally well on those operations in the Occupied Territories, except for a single case: I was supposed to locate the

Noam Chayut

home of someone wanted by the Shabak, but it simply vanished
from the village after I made a wrong turn.

I closed the old notebook and drew a new one out of my
pack. I wrote "Crisis Management" in large letters on the
front. And by the time the plane had touched down in Israel,
I already had a whole set of rules noted down that would
prevent me from wallowing in sorrow. They stipulated a tight
daily schedule:

06:00 wake up
06:30–07:30 morning run on the beach
07:30–08:00 morning swim (this was in mid-winter)
08:30–09:30 reading a book in English in preparation for
    my university entrance exams (+one cigarette)
10:00–10:30 breakfast, up to 500 calories (veggies, 2
    crackers with cheese, hard-boiled egg, 1 teaspoon olive
    oil)
10:30–12:30 studying for the exams (+15 minute coffee-
    cigarette break)
12:30–13:30 free time (may be extended to 2 hours only
    if meeting with friends)
13:30–15:30 studying Hebrew for the exams (+15 minutes
    coffee-cigarette break)
15:30 fruit snack
15:35–16:30 free time (if previous break was 2 hours, this
    one is off)
16:30–17:00 walk outdoors (+cigarette)
17:00–18:00 English reading

166

18:00–19:00 supper, up to 600 calories for the first fort-
night, up to 1,100 calories later on (+15 minutes
coffee-cigarette break)
19:00–19:30 cold shower
And so on and so forth, continuing various "tasks" until
lights out at precisely 23:00.

Below the schedule were "points of emphasis to be carried out":

- no television of any kind (not even in my free time
  slots, nor films nor watching at friends' homes with
  them);
- masturbate no more than 3 times a day and only in my
  free time slots;
- one beer (half a liter) allowed every other day, calories
  taken off the supper dose;
- weigh-in every Sunday at 06:00, note results in graph
  form;
- number of cigarettes pre-set every morning, not to be
  changed;

With time, more items were added: a theater workshop twice a
week; laughing meditation (you should try it: sit alone indoors
or out, and begin to laugh stupidly, until your inhibition is
broken and you are rolling with laughter; it's amazingly liberating). A daily chore was added as well: taking a dog out on Tel
Aviv's Basel Street. The names on its owner's door were Maya
and Mika, or the other way around, and I can't remember

which was the lawyer and which the dog. The pay hardly covered gas but I didn't care.

I was busy for seventeen hours a day with self-improvement and not thinking about anything.

I drew a graph with the X coordinate representing weeks and the Y coordinate representing my weight in kilos. I lost ten kilos surprisingly fast, and another eight hiking the Israel Trail. I was feeling too thin for the first time in my life.

On the phone, Yehuda spoke about his plan to put up an exhibition of photographs taken in Hebron by soldiers during their military service. The exhibition would also include video projections in which soldiers of his company and other companies would give personal testimony, telling what madness it was to be a combatant in Hebron. I suppose that, had he said Jenin or Nablus or the whole West Bank instead of Hebron, I would have waved the madman away and sent him off. First of all, it didn't sound to me like something anyone would even agree to hear. Secondly, I was deep into the last week of my regimen, which was growing more and more sophisticated with time: I had begun to list precise breakfast ingredients, the number of allowed cigarettes three days in advance, book titles and page numbers to be read, times at which to call close friends and the allowed length of the conversations, as well as time for push-ups, sit-ups and pull-ups. When it was possible, I would even write and map out my dreams.

But Yehuda had said "Hebron," and I could hardly wave that off.

*　　*　　*

Of my three years as an officer in the Occupied Territories, I spent only three weeks in Hebron. But in those three weeks— although I still had faith in the system, thought it was absolutely necessary, and believed in my proper and important role within it—I simply couldn't believe what I saw.

During one of my foot patrols there, I had a childish idea that I mulled over several times: I would go on television and tell the nation what was happening in Hebron. I imagined myself being interviewed on prime-time TV, telling how the Jewish settlers beat up Palestinian passers-by, threw stones at them and damaged their property and homes. How the settler children harassed local families under curfew, and what violent, crass language they used with soldiers. I had no doubt that if sane people in this country only knew what went on in Hebron, public opinion would not allow it to continue. I had a plan to tape events on video and distribute them as soon as I got out of the army. But this did not happen; even my normal still camera bears not a trace of Hebron.

I spent such a short time in Hebron only because when I got there with my battalion, an officer was needed for several weeks on a rear job: navigation tutoring for the brigade's officer course candidates. And perhaps because I nagged my superiors with questions about the necessity of our missions there, and became a real nuisance at staff meetings, I was assigned to the training base and my own platoon was left in the hands of my sergeant. When the navigation training was over, my battalion was already assigned to Jenin and we never went back to Hebron.

Yehuda Shaul said he wished to interview me in order to "bring Hebron to Tel Aviv, speak here about what happens there."

I remembered the childish idea I had had during my patrols in the city, so I couldn't refuse him. When he arrived, I was all packed for my trek and was just sitting down to my 1,100-calorie supper.

He arrived on a small motorcycle, a heavy, bearded fellow with a large black skullcap, wielding an impressive video camera. He entered and asked only for some water. Perspiring, he installed his camera on a tripod placed opposite me and proceeded to present his ideas. He didn't have a coherent plan yet, but he had plenty of vision and faith. I also realized that this pleasant, polite and easygoing person was an irresistible bulldozer. Eventually, I would have the privilege of getting to know him very well—his capacity to listen, his willingness to make decisions only after consulting his partners in the organization and reaching unanimity, for which endless discussion and mutual persuasion were often needed. It became a privilege to know him and work with him.

But that evening he only asked me to tell him what I had seen, experienced and felt in Hebron. I said I had been there for a very short time and merely described two short incidents about which I wished to testify.

In one, a group of settler children threw stones, hit with sticks and swore at an old Arab woman as she climbed steep Shuhada Street, heavily laden with shopping baskets. When we rushed to her rescue, they cursed us too. On the other occasion, a little Jewish child threw a pomegranate that he had picked from a tree at the window of a Palestinian family. The family members, bound by curfew, stood helpless behind their windows. It was my first day in Hebron, and we were making the rounds of the army posts with the force we had come to replace. The child stood just a few meters away from me.

I approached him and gripped his shoulder with the instinct of an adult catching a kid red-handed. From the corner of my eye I saw two settlers approaching. I thought, here come two responsible adults who will chastise him. But no, as they arrived they rained curses on me: Nazi, wimp, stupid leftie in soldier guise. They even spat at me. I was stunned.

Later that evening I recalled the long lecture I got from my mother when it became known in our village that kids hurled pomegranates from the basketball court, close to The Stone, at the home of the old Frankel couple. I was not one of the throwers; I was little and hardly ever allowed to set foot on that court. It was the bigger kids' kind of prank. At most, my age group would throw pine cones at the home of Tzipa the Witch, and only after we made sure she was seen carrying her basket on the way to the grocery store. Tearful, I had to confess that I was there on the court and saw it all. I even named some of the older kids who led the pomegranate-throwing. For this "singing" I later got slapped and punched in the face, just as at another occasion I received a "wooden leg"—a knee thrust into my thigh—from another boy. A wooden leg is quite painful, nearly as painful as the feeling you have crying in front of everybody.

171

I would again encounter a wooden leg in the Palestinian city of Ramallah. We were enforcing a curfew. A Border Patrolman under my command had just treated a Palestinian truck driver to a wooden leg. I announced at our briefing that if I caught a soldier hitting a Palestinian, he would end up in jail. I swore by my mother and her mother that this was exactly what I would do. Afterwards, the Border Patrol commander on the ground informed me, in his cynically official tone, that they were at my command, or as he put it: "Cool man. Whatever you say. This is your designated area. No hitting, but no curfew either. Let's see you handle it by yourself, sir." Then he added, between his teeth while boarding the Jeep: "Sss . . . yellow infantryman."

"Yellow" in army jargon meant wimp; it was no longer some ethnic invective referring to hair color, but rather a description of behavior. The opposite of "yellow" in this slang was, surprisingly, "Arab": strong, violent, tough. It was a real honor to be tagged a company of "Arabs." As a result, perversely, "Arab" is pejorative when meaning a "local," a Palestinian, but an honor when describing a soldier or Border Patrolman.

We patrolled with that Border Patrol crew several more times, and once I heard one of them saying, "Don't touch anyone near that yellow guy with the beard." I felt moral, righteous even. A part of the "Enlightened Occupation." Clearly, behind my back a lot of beatings were taking place. Obviously, too, the Border Patrol officer was right: without brute force we had to use much more teargas and rubber ammo, and curfew was not successfully enforced. The truth is that the only moral thing I could have done was share with my superiors the insight that curfew cannot be enforced without systematically violating all the orders regarding our treatment of civilians. And that I was going home to look for another kind of life. I didn't. It didn't even cross my mind. On the contrary: I felt I was an enlightened person, belonging to the most moral army in the world . . .

The two testimonies I gave Yehuda Shaul that evening were similar in essence to most of the other testimonies later projected at the exhibition: stories that blamed others, usually settlers, or sometimes the sheer force of circumstance. But there were a few testimonies of another kind: deeper, not merely dry descriptions of unpleasant sights, but stories dealing with feelings and emotions, admitting personal responsibility, engaging in self-reflection. These were testimonies of combatants who even during their service realized that they were responsible, that their actions enabled the existence of that whole surreal apparatus that totally paralyzed life in the center of a big city while serving a few hundred settlers.

Only by seeing these testimonies did I realize that during my own service, my understanding of the situation was paltry compared to theirs. I had been ignorant. Even when I got annoyed with a settler child throwing a pomegranate at the window of a poor family trapped helplessly in its own home, I never thought of my own role in this scenario. It never crossed my mind that this child could only harass them, in fact, because

I was standing there and protecting him, as well as enforcing the curfew upon them.

Even at the exhibition in Tel Aviv, I told one of the interviewers who had asked me about my military service that I thought the IDF was the most moral army in the world: "It's not the army that should be judged, but the society that sends it on its missions."

On the videotapes from that exhibition, our words and even our body language were instructive. My reserve battalion commander was right about me: I was still a soldier in spirit. A few days after the exhibition I was interviewed on Israel Radio 2 opposite a settler woman in charge of education in the Jewish settlement of Hebron. I was sharp and convincing in this interview, just as I had daydreamed of being on my Hebron patrol. Many people called up to congratulate me, and one friend even joined Breaking the Silence as a result. But that was still the easy phase, a verbal media confrontation with a settler on a radio station highly favoring the Israeli soldier. I had not yet reached my own revelation.

CHAPTER 23

When Yehuda Shaul looked in the mirror after his discharge, he did not see the smiling orthodox-religious boy who loved to hike throughout the country and help the needy. He saw a monster terrorizing the streets of Hebron. He was horrified at his own image. Why him of all people?

Maybe because he did not grow up with my Holocaust. For him, enlisting in the army was a breech of social custom among the religious circles of his own youth. Perhaps this was his reason for discovering the monster on the day of his discharge, the moment he turned in his army gear.

Yehuda Shaul is not a normal person. Instead of going to a shrink or wiping his mind clean with drugs in India, or suppressing and denying and waiting for the day it would all burst out, he roared: "If I look in the mirror and see a monster, then every member of the society that sent me must see this monster, too. I will show it."

And so he did.

CHAPTER 24

The photo exhibition "Breaking the Silence—Combatants Talk about Hebron" opened in June 2004 at the College for Geographic Photography in Tel Aviv. It struck some shrill notes and generated a vigorous public response. One day the Military Police arrived and confiscated videotapes and testimonies. The three organizers of the exhibition had all served in Hebron: Yehuda, a large, heavy-set ultra-orthodox graduate of a *yeshivah* high school in the Occupied Territories; Jonas, a good-looking, tall and slender fellow with long sideburns like a '70s rock star, who was a well-mannered counselor of a Zionist youth movement group; and Micha, a noisy, funny type, short with dark curls, who believed in a fair autarchic economy and justice for all. They were interrogated and warned about their own part in the so-called crimes they were exposing. This only highlighted the absurd situation: having shown people what we have been doing for the past forty years, the organizers were investigated by the army for just that—brutally enforcing curfew, shooting at street lamps and hurling teargas canisters into schoolhouse windows.

It was an attempt to intimidate us and, I admit, they certainly managed to intimidate me. I got scared and went north for a few days to wait out the storm. But the army's attempt to scare us had the opposite effect: it gave the exhibition excellent publicity and drew thousands of visitors. In time I came to my senses, returned and gradually became involved in the movement as it was forming.

When the exhibition was over, a group of us sat together and planned our next activity. Along with a team of ten veterans, we had documentary filmmaker Avi Mugrabi and press photographer Miki Kratzman, both weathered activists in the Territories. They consulted and supported us, and they were wise enough to let us go through our own process at our own pace. If they had given us their opinions and worldview to begin with, I probably would have left the group.

Before I lost my Holocaust I would not have understood lunatics such as Avi Mugrabi. Yet I myself brought up militant ideas for what to do next, although I am not at all sure I would have had the guts to carry them out. I suggested, for example, that we drive around in my Subaru jalopy and with a large loudspeaker announce curfew on well-to-do northern Tel Aviv neighborhoods, put up roadblocks in Israeli towns and replicate other such features of Occupation. Miki curbed my enthusiasm, suggesting we appear not as court jesters but as a serious organization with new information and a novel, harsh statement.

I don't know what would have happened had we chosen the prank route, but after seeing how four Special Forces policemen beat anarchists to a pulp in a 2006 demonstration protesting the Second Lebanon War, I'm glad we did not take that path. I have seen much violence in my days—beatings, stone throwing, Molotov cocktails, drunks fighting on the dance floor—but the sight of four huge police thugs furiously beating up a sixteen-year-old girl armed with only a squeaky voice and a camera made me realize that I hadn't really known true violence. One huge guy bent her arm backward, two others lifted her legs and a fourth punched her with his fists. Her protest shouts became agonized screams and they, who didn't even perspire, laughed out loud. All this happened in front of my eyes as I looked on from a safe distance in a particularly rich neighborhood of lovely Tel Aviv.

To avoid being beaten by the "black shirts," one must move away slowly from the middle of a demonstration and stand off quietly, just as one does when facing a fang-baring dog—don't run, don't look in its eyes, stand still, lower your gaze and pray.

The activities we decided to focus on included gathering testimonies from veterans and from soldiers still serving. We would record interviews with the soldiers, publish these testimonies as booklets, and hold lectures for the general public and in homes, where we would tell the story of our organization and present the testimonies we had gathered. In addition, we would put up a website and post the testimonies. We also took it upon ourselves to pass our tougher episodes on to the media whenever possible.

CHAPTER 25

In most interviews, the witness is at an initial phase of shedding his faith in the system, in the myth of the humane fighter serving in a moral army. It is an unconscious process that sometimes takes years. But sometimes it also stops there, for there are those who, having given testimony, go back to where they came from, to unanimously accepted norms, their previous beliefs and views. Witnesses give testimony for various reasons: for some, truth itself is important, while some see testifying as a political act, and others seek their little private revenge against the system. Some do not always understand what the whole racket is about—when a friend asks them to tell a story, they simply tell it. Others cannot keep still and have no idea why. And there are many whose motives I just couldn't figure out.

After conducting many interviews, one learns to recognize repeated behavior patterns of the testifying soldiers. On the phone or at a first encounter, the fellow hurriedly tells you he is not sure that making these things public is the right thing to do—people might be hurt, and the truth is that he doesn't have that much to tell and it's a waste of my time, and if I come I'll be disappointed. "But if you really want this, we could talk for a few minutes." These minutes usually turn into long hours.

At the second meeting, which is the recording session, there are many who apologize again for the trouble I've taken to reach them, for they have no horror stories to tell. Usually this sentence is said with a lowered gaze. Then, as the fellow makes coffee, I tell him about the organization and explain the significance of the recorded interview. I assure him that he has personal immunity through journalistic confidentiality, and that his name and other personal information will be kept secret by us, unless he wishes to reveal them. On the other hand, we are unable to protect others whom he might name. Therefore he better not name his mates and superiors, only their roles and ranks.

The first question posed at the interview: Is there anything that weighs on you, something in particular you'd like to tell us? In answer, the interviewee usually tells one story that he has prepared, the only one he has intended to disclose.

"My own conscience is clear, and anyway I couldn't have made much of a difference."

This is, more or less, how he will open. Obeying a healthy natural defense mechanism, he will deny personal responsibility for things that might prove painful or even unbearable to account for.

Then he will tell the story he has prepared: an act of looting or harassment, vandalism or killing, playing with dead bodies or a violent arrest, the use of a human shield or the ransacking of a home—a precise description of one event deeply etched in his memory. More seldom, that first story will crack some hidden dam and be followed by a flood of descriptions and events disconnected in time and place. But the narrator will always repeat emphatically that he had no pull, no say in the matter.

If he recounts an event he witnessed from the outside—like the one I told Yehuda about the settler children—the matter is clear-cut and simple. If he speaks about an incident in which he took part, he will say he had no choice, circumstances technical or otherwise could not be altered. Only a few of the witnesses, mostly peace- or social activists, will accompany their testimony—bitterly or ironically delivered—with explicit feelings of repentance and shame. Even a company commander who testified about a tank firing from inside his army position into a city, killing an entire family, opened by saying his conscience was clear. The force of this mechanism—the protestation of innocence that protects our psyche from the harsh facts—is undoubtedly one of the wonders of the human brain. The man was the senior officer on the ground and even issued the order himself. And he was still sure that this killing was not his responsibility.

When the army spokesperson later announced that a family had accidentally been killed, the Minister of Defense apologized and the army expressed regret for its error. The press reported: "An IDF tank shell hit the vehicle of a senior Hamas official and killed his wife, their three little children and another two girls in the next car. The Hamas member himself was not inside the car . . ." And that company commander didn't even consider revealing the truth: that there was no attempt at "targeted killing" but rather a fiasco, a "wandering shell" as the saying goes. And the shell was to blame.

He did not consider saying that an order was issued (very high up the ranks) to kill Palestinian uniformed officials as a retaliatory measure. That some gunner in the tank did not want to kill an unarmed traffic policeman and so aimed at the hills, out of town. Or probably some "yellow" gunner missed on purpose. And there was the commander who was peeved by this kind of pussyfooting, so he got into the gunner's seat himself, aimed at the policeman poised on the roundabout— whistle in his mouth, hand raised in that asinine gesture of traffic policemen—and also missed, hitting a car that was just then rounding the bend. Rumor has it that the gunner later climbed out of the tank and carved swastikas on his body with a knife and perhaps even yelled "I'm a Nazi!"

The company commander, our witness, was in his post the whole time, more or less aware of this chain of events, and he did not report it to anyone. Instead, he read about it in the papers and even then did not say a word. And still he did not regard himself as an accomplice in any act of whitewashing. The army spokesperson can count on us, field men, to keep quiet. This time, too, none of the combatants would expose the lie. For whoever talks might possibly incriminate himself, and even if not, he might be held accountable for lethal, unbearable complicity.

And what about the public? The public went on believing that this was a failed attempt on the life of a Hamas operative about to commit a terrorist bombing—that this is a "no choice" war, that our soldiers are the most moral in the world.

No thought was given to the person who did the actual shooting, to the fact that such killing may have wrought havoc in his psyche.

We finished recording very late and he offered me some more black coffee before my drive back to Beer Sheva. We began a kind of talk—well, just a nominal one—about feelings of responsibility and repentance: "Look," he said. "I did everything I could. I mean, true, I didn't report the incident to anyone, but I was still in the army at the time, it's not done, and even . . . Maybe I do have a part in this but . . . perhaps I could have done something . . . I didn't think this way back then . . . I don't know."

Nor did I.

CHAPTER 26

During the exhibition, a very special interviewee came my way: one who invented himself, fictionalized his own image. It was early on, and I was not sufficiently familiar with the various behavior patterns of our witnesses to realize something here was not quite right. This chap showed not a moment's hesitation before agreeing to testify.

He didn't say his conscience was clear. Nor did he express any regrets or feelings of guilt. He made no introductions but went ahead and told the one story he had prepared. After telling it, he was unwilling to add anything, not even about the rest of his military service.

"Where did your unit proceed from there?"

"Where else were you assigned?"

"What kinds of training did you have?"

I tried to insist, and he—nothing. He evaded it all. I had to make do with his personal information: name, serial number, date of enlistment and unit. At my request, he left a phone number. I called, a recording answered: "Cellcom, hello—this call cannot be completed as dialed. Please check the number and dial again . . ."

Okay, I thought, he must have been distracted as he wrote down his number for me.

A little while later, an ex-girlfriend suggested I interview an acquaintance of hers. As chance would have it, he had enlisted together with my disappearing witness, and had even served in the same unit. I pitied him for having to carry around such a terrible story, and I hoped he himself was not a direct accomplice. His testimony was quite routine. He had prepared a few stories in advance, and then indulged me and described his whole army career, thereby recalling other events in the process. Like all witnesses, he had some emotional moments as he spoke — of excitement, regret, fear of implicating his mates. He expressed the confusion common to people describing crimes they had witnessed — "crimes" was the word he himself used — mostly committed by people he loved and appreciated and sometimes even admired.

He spoke for some time but sensed that I expected more, something greater. He asked if I was disappointed, if I thought he was wasting my time, as he had warned me earlier. Indeed, I expected more because I imagined he was concealing or even suppressing the story of that other witness from his own company. I tried to take him back to the city where that event had supposedly taken place.

"Did anything else happen there that we may have skipped?"

"Not that I recall, no."

I had no choice. I switched the recorder off to make him feel more at ease, and mentioned the event the other witness had spoken about. No, he knew nothing about that, he said.

185

He added that nothing of that sort could have possibly taken place in his company without him hearing of it.

Further checks showed that the dates the other witness had mentioned did not coincide with the time their company had served in the place where the incident supposedly took place. But this could still have been explained as an honest error committed while reconstructing dates.

Then I asked him outright whether he knew the fellow whose name was written in my notebook next to the phone number that proved to be wrong.

"Listen, we never had anyone with that name in our company."

"Eh?"

"If we did, I would know him. I was there the whole time. You think I'd 'accidentally' not know someone who enlisted with me in a paratroopers company?"

"No."

It really made no sense. I checked his enlistment again and the name of the company, noted below his name and phone number, and found no explanation. At the group's next meeting, Miki suggested the only logical explanation: someone had "planted" this witness in order to trip us. After the details of his story were published, it would be very easy to refute and thereby stain our whole endeavor. We were a group of innocent, inexperienced young people facing . . . I didn't really know whom and what, but we did learn our lesson then, that this someone or something did not always believe in fair play.

CHAPTER 27

In my search for testimonies, one of the first things I did was to call a friend of mine from my own team on our recon company. I'll call him "the guy." As I was sent to officers' training, I left our team about two months after we had finished our specialization. For that interim we had little to do in the Occupied Territories and plenty of time to kill. Those were the first days following the Israeli army's retreat from Lebanon and our unit, like many others, lay nearly idle.

The missions we did carry out were localized, like arresting men wanted by the Shabak or setting ambushes for intelligence gathering—assignments I would define as military compared to the violent policing actions enforcing military law upon civilian population which I would have to perform later in my service. I remember that on one of those intelligence gathering missions, the information was meant to help assassinate a Palestinian who had killed a Jewish settler from Hebron in what the brigade intelligence personnel called a "land feud." "If we manage to take him down thanks to information you'll bring in," the brigade intelligence officer urged us, "that would be the nicest gift we could give the Jewish settlers in Hebron for the coming holiday."

In October 2000, when the present bloodshed began, I was already in officers' training. "The guy," along with the rest of my team, had about another year until their discharge, and during that year they functioned like other regular forces implementing orders that were becoming gradually more extreme throughout the West Bank and Gaza Strip. At the time, my officers' course mates, me included, were alerted to the Kisufim crossing (Gaza Strip). From there we would occasionally go on security patrols on the road leading to the settlements of the Qatif block. But most of the time we sat around our APCs, bored, waiting to be summoned. Then we began to lay nightly ambushes, waiting to catch the men who set explosive charges on the route, uproot numerous olive trees on "razing" missions, and in daytime just chat around and joke, usually while humiliating Palestinian passers-by.

In our endless free time we ate tons of snacks that were handed out free, smoked Noblesse and Time cigarettes, also free handouts—war is war, after all—and in between sex-talk, the blues, solitude and homesickness, we told each other about our friends in our original units: what was going on in *Duvdevan** and other various recon units, and in the infantry battalions of Golani and the paratroopers. How many have they managed to kill and where. Like everyone, I too would repeatedly phone my teammates to inquire where and how many.

---

* Undercover squad.

During the first month of the confrontation, Palestinian rage was directed at both the army and settlers. The initial score in this game, before the terrorist bombings that followed shortly afterwards, was 0:100, namely we killed 100 Palestinians and they killed none of our men. This made us very proud; our commander at officers' training course assembled us and explained that after the "Wailing Wall Tunnel events" of 1996, when sixteen soldiers were killed within just a few days, the army has gotten better organized, secured itself and prepared, and these are the results – one hundred to zero. His speech was delivered in typical "officer-talk" mode, including phrases such as "Our actions are carried out in total synergy versus the sporadic fire encountered on the ground."

The guys, including myself, were busy counting the Xs marked by our mother-unit peers, competing over whose unit had killed more Palestinians. One of my teammates told me on the phone that my recon recruits of March 1999, four months younger than my own team, had killed so and so many. Every casualty of the enemy won them an X, and in some units the X would be etched on the magazine that contained the lethal bullet. I clearly remember envying the March 1999 recruits. They were just a few kilometers down the road from me at the Qatif Block Junction inside the Gaza strip itself, and most of their marksmen already sported Xs.

We all wanted to take part in the fighting. Such was the spirit, the talk of the day. When soldiers younger than ourselves—fresher into the service—killed and rushed off to tell their mates, and we were just on standby, bored, next to our APC, gear in hand, we felt totally humiliated.

Three years later I called "the guy" from my own team and asked him to tell me the tales of those combats and X markings. He was not eager to talk. As a person, he had clear-cut political and social awareness, siding with ideas of partitioning the land as a solution to the conflict, believing in respect for human rights, in short an idealist—one who planned a career in education because he saw it as the sole answer to all our problems. This in mind, I could hardly understand why he did not want to testify.

First he said he had heard me on radio, read about the exhibition in the press as well as watched the first exposure of *Breaking the Silence* on Israel TV Channel 2's highest-rated fact-finding program. And still, although he generally agreed with our goals, he found things a bit risky. One couldn't know whom this information could serve in the future. I assured him that the organization provided top confidentiality but he still refused; and I wouldn't relent. I pressured him until he disclosed his real reason:

"You guys are dealing with checkpoints and curfew and humiliation and other such bullshit. We were not a part of all that. My stories deal with human lives, do you understand what I'm saying? I'm talking to you about murder. Murder."

His voice was tense, and the word murder that he repeated still rang strange in my testimony-gathering vocabulary. I had not yet heard it. "If that's what you have to tell, then obviously you must expose it," I answered.

"You don't really understand, do you? These are guys from our own team I'm talking about."

Again I assured him that no one would have direct access to the original text of his testimony and the team mentioned would not be identified. Nor will any soldier be implicated simply for being involved.

"But they will know and I don't intend to speak."

"And your fear of embarrassing a chum is more important than the public's right to know about a murder? Does that make sense?"

But at this point the dialogue ended. We exchanged some more polite words, and finished off, never to speak together again. I was disappointed with the guy, as well as with myself. I had failed; I had brought to light none of my team's doings in the Occupied Territories while I had been away in officers' training. My contact with them has slackened since then. At first I didn't show up at team get-togethers, then I felt out of place at their weddings, and finally I was no longer invited anyway.

But I still think about that guy sometimes. He was wise and kind, and I have no doubt that if his conscience was weighed down by tales of murder, he was tormented. People of his sort, feeling they have complied with crimes, pay a heavy emotional price if they don't break the silence, even if only not to bear this burden alone.

CHAPTER 28

I gathered many testimonies, and listened to others gathered by my friends. In the first months, I was stunned by the dimensions of violence and humiliation they revealed. The excuse of "rotten apples" within the "moral occupation" cart disappeared. In its stead, a whole system of organized evil was revealed. My own process of shedding my previous self was now leaping from one testimony to the next.

The interviews were accumulating, gradually constructing the simple story of Breaking the Silence as a movement: recording the Occupation as told from the occupier's point of view—the point of view of soldiers who served in the Occupied Territories since the outbreak of the Second Intifada in October 2000. These were the stories of frightened boys who commanded checkpoints, enforced curfews, and patrolled streets and markets. These were the stories of the indifference and numbness they developed there, which swallowed up their own personalities.

The soldiers' truthful accounts reflected the lives of Palestinians, many of whom for the last forty years have never spent a single night without the possibility that twenty khaki-clad fellows might bang on their door in the middle of the night, turn their home inside out, search, rummage, confiscate, lock the whole family in one room and do whatever they pleased. Such testimonies shocked me only when they accumulated in large quantity—only when I could draw similarities between them and guess the testifier's next sentence, even if I was not familiar with his designated area or unit.

But there were some individual testimonies that affected me personally. For example, there was a sensitive chap whom I didn't even need to provoke into confession. The moment I posed my opening question, he opened up and told me in one fell swoop of six different incidents, all of which ended with the death of innocents.

He used the word "murder," and at some point even admitted through his gestures that perhaps he himself had pulled the trigger, although he took it back immediately. Choking, his eyes damp, he said it could have been any other soldier who was there. Yet he also said he felt like a murderer walking free—and I could hardly tone down his harsh self-accusations. After their deaths, he and his fellow soldiers gave nicknames to all six casualties in his testimony, just like in the well-known poem by the celebrated Israeli poet Zelda Schneersohn Mishkovsky: "Everyone has a name given by one's death." His unit-mates produced a morbid burlesque depicting those nightly operations, including songs set to music about them.

One of them was "the kid," for the victim was a little kid who moved a plastic roadblock in the middle of the street.

He jeopardized absolutely no one, but moving that road-block meant death by live gunfire. A bullet hit his chest and he was killed on the spot. The real name of that child was Hani Qandul, according to an investigation carried out by *Yedioth Aharonot* newspaper following our testimony-gathering.

The next victim received the nickname "the baker," for he was holding a bag full of flatbreads when he was killed. He was on his way back from the bakery at dawn, when bakers do their work so that we all have fresh bread when we get up in the morning. Orders were to "shoot to kill" anyone seen walking in the street between this and that hour in this and that designated zone. The man with the flatbread, who knew nothing about the rules of engagement, suited that scheme perfectly and was therefore shot and killed by the book. A frag grenade was used for the "confirm-kill" procedure, which left a lot of shrapnel in the fresh flatbreads. No one ate them, not even the legal heirs of the late "baker." Summing up the operation, the commander reassured the soldiers: "Whoever wanders around outdoors at such an hour obviously has a terrorist agenda."

The gang's next victim received the name "the old man," simply because he was elderly. He died of a heart attack when a team of our boys broke in to his home.

"The lookout": this was the fourth victim's nickname. He was taken down because he stood on a roof holding a mobile phone. He was unarmed, but the boys had explicit instructions to finish him off. Anyone standing on a roof holding a cell phone is clearly a lookout gathering and passing on information about the Israeli army forces in his neighborhood. He is thus sentenced to death by shooting.

Imagine for a moment that you live in a rooftop apartment or at least have a large roof veranda, and are calling your mom to tell her she has nothing to worry about. Yes, there was a bombing on the next street over, but you are alright. You were sitting in your living room at the time and you are perfectly fine. "And now all's well. Yes, your grandchildren are asleep. That's why I went outside to call you, although it's cold. It took a while to put the little one down. She always notices tension and starts crying and can't fall asleep. But thank goodness, Mom, we're fine. No, we're not going out, no way. We've got all we need. We have food in the house for at least a week. Go to sleep, Mom, everything will be fine. There's really nothing to worry about. It's all quiet now. Yes . . ."

Did she hear the shot? The fall? And who found her son dead on the roof? Did he realize he was gone?

Or perhaps "the lookout" was not calming his mother. Maybe he was a lookout indeed, even busy passing on information to the enemy. Perhaps, but unlikely. I believe the statistics were in his favor: in a city under fire, most phone conversations taking place inside are not likely to serve combat purposes. Unlikely. I haven't checked. But what I do know today is that the echelons issuing that order never bothered to think about it. They wanted casualties. Palestinians. A lot. And yes, they wanted every killing to have a suitable military justification.

The fifth victim was nicknamed "the drummer." Islamic tradition dominates North Africa and the entire Middle East all the way to Iran—except for a tiny Jewish enclave on the shores of the Mediterranean. It also reaches east to Afghanistan and Pakistan, and has an arm stretching from Syria over to Asian Turkey, at the gates of Christian Europe. It is also practiced in various other spots around the globe such as Malaysia and Kerala—the Indian state where I am now.

If you've heard anything about that tradition, you certainly know that it sanctifies one special month: Ramadan, when Muslims fast from dawn to dusk. Throughout this month they pray a lot, abstain from smoking during daytime, refrain from sexual intercourse and observe all religious rulings even more carefully than usual. In those regions, a nice, friendly custom is observed: at dawn, representatives of the community, at the bidding of the local mosque, go forth and make noise in the streets to wake up the lazy still wallowing in bed, reminding them this is their last opportunity to eat their fill before the sun rises and their day-long fast begins. In those pre-dawn hours, the interviewee's team walked in the dark on its nightly routine mission. And there, right ahead, emerged a figure holding a large object, looking suspicious and scary.

Not a single one of the team members was familiar with the custom. Truth be told, they didn't even know it was Ramadan. The end was already obvious—death by shooting. The fellow out on the street holding a large drum—like the kid, like the baker and the lookout—was at the wrong place at the wrong time, and he too was shot and killed. By sun-up he even had a name: "the drummer."

Or as the refrain goes, in the song that the combatants set to music:

> *Another pediatrician,*
> *And baker*
> *Got shot in the face*
> *By us paratroopers.*
> *All day we search their homes*
> *And kill children.*

This morbid humor must have made its way up the chain of command, from the privates to the company officers. In the inquiry held after one of these operations, the operations officer concluded his report by writing: "lessons to be learned: there must be no killing of innocents."

Nice, don't you think?

The sixth victim was "the woman."

The witness who described these six cases also described military routine at checkpoints: one must never know in advance who is entitled to get through, and even if you do, it is hard to remember because there are innumerable types of permits and they change very frequently. Sometimes they expire even before the permit-holder manages to reach the checkpoint.

In this context, he spoke about a chapter in a project his mother, a historian, wrote about Nazi Germany before the extermination of the Jews. In Germany back then, one needed documents for everything—certificates and permits whose validity would expire shortly after being issued: "The rules would change so that it became impossible to follow them, and this was done merely to exhaust the Jewish population." And the witness apologized: "I'm not comparing, but . . ." And he compared.

Still, he thought his younger brother should become a combatant and not dodge his military duty, as "there is no other way." This opinion he expressed just moments after depicting the Occupied Territories as the "Wild West," where any commander does whatever he likes, unharnessed, ruthless.

At first I felt sorry for him, but a few days later I began to feel sorry for myself as well, for all of us. While walking the streets of Germany at the age of sixteen, as one of the many who still had their Holocaust, like all my fellow mission members at the time, I looked at elderly Germans and wondered what they were or did back then, in those dark times. Our delegation was on a friendship mission, so we learned a lot about Germans who resisted the Nazis: communists, anarchists, liberals and human rights activists who, like the numerous members of my Labendik family, were tortured and murdered by that apparatus. Look at that grandpa, I would think. He may have lost his entire world because one of his family members or even he himself resisted the regime.

But perhaps he was a Nazi, or a soldier of the Wehrmacht, or perhaps—most likely—just one of the "silent majority." After that testimony, I began to look at my peers in Israel and wonder what they had done—and especially, how did they feel? Did they regard themselves as murderers? If not now, will they see themselves that way in the future?

And what about me? I was simply lucky: as far as I knew, I managed not to kill anyone myself, with my own hands, before I woke up. This lightens my sense of complicity in killing. When I look at myself in the mirror, right in the eyes, I don't really understand what I'm seeing. But when I look around me, I see the silent majority. Silent not only in the face of the everyday killing and suffering in the Occupied Territories, but also towards this fellow and those like him, who went forth on behalf of society and now, back from combat, feel they've committed crimes, feel that they are accomplices to "executions performed under immoral orders, and I think, illegal orders as well . . ." These were his very words.

CHAPTER 29

The testimony about the six killings, like other testimonies about killings from different units and designated areas, were to be published in the weekend supplement of *Yedioth Aharonot*. This popular newspaper got scared at the last moment, halted the planned promos and nearly regretted its decision to publish the story. But it was ultimately published, so hundreds of thousands of people received the testimonies on their very doorstep. We hectically prepared ourselves for the day after publication. We assigned each other to be interviewed. We discussed how we would react to every possible response. We rounded up all our activists who were willing and capable of speaking. We drew lessons from previous interviews and memorized our message: these are by no means "exceptional cases" or "rotten apples." We have shown the public the rules and regulations that bring about excessive, superfluous bloodshed among the inhabitants of the Occupied Territories, so that the public will know, and can criticize, this overall corruption of morals.

And the day after? Nothing happened. Unlike the racket raised throughout the country when we exposed episodes of looting, vandalism and humiliation some months earlier, these stories, so much harsher, went down with hardly a ripple. We were not summoned for interviews by other media, and no substantial public discussion was held. Why? How could this huge scandal just dissipate like some tiny stinky fart, disappearing into thin air?

Because no one was willing to confront the matter of executions and orders. And when no one is eager to argue, discuss and be interviewed, the whole issue evaporates. In the military system's list of moral justifications, this series of killings had no ready explanation. Checkpoint stories could always be explained away by saying that the commander went overboard, acted under duress, hit the roof. Looting episodes could be presented as exceptions, or one could claim that the money was not stolen but confiscated because it was intended to finance terrorism. Acts of brutality while enforcing curfew, and humiliation and beatings of shackled prisoners, are regarded as wild flukes to be dealt with harshly. And when a human shield was injured, one could report that "uninvolved" persons accidentally happened upon the scene.

But the series we produced, which I've retitled in my own mind "An Innocent Shot and Killed by the Book," and which we also published as a booklet, could not be dismissed so easily. It featured testimonies from soldiers in numerous units, youngsters who became killers by force of the rules of engagement, which amounted to killing for killing's sake — such facts could not be explained away by the usual *hasbara* and advocacy tricks. No denials would work here: the perpetrators themselves were the speakers. One could not call them "rotten apples"—there were too many of them. Responsibility could not be deflected to scapegoats on trial, because investigations would soon enough lead to the higher echelons: commanders of battalions, brigades, regional commands, even to the chief of staff himself.

And when there's no way to deal with a matter, it's better not to deal with it. The lack of any response is a winning response for the system because it ignites no flames. Over the years, the army's non-reaction has been refined to such a degree that if a soldier or ex-officer representing Breaking the Silence is interviewed on a subject, the military will decline to be interviewed on the same subject. Since the reporter cannot, then, balance the discussion, he is usually forced to cancel the story and the testimonies are silenced yet again.

CHAPTER 30

Yehuda Shaul once interviewed an army driver who had no dramatic events to recount. He was not a combatant during most of his service, and in his testimony he relied mostly on rumors he heard in his battalion—an "atmosphere interview" is how we referred to it.

He said, for example, that their battalion commander would assemble his men and try to "poison" them, as army lingo has it. This meant that he would motivate them, encourage them and ratchet up their fighting spirit. The commander told the soldiers that he knew they were just dying to kill Arabs, to tear them to pieces. But, he added, "We must hold back now, for those are our orders. So don't be upset. I, too, long to kill Arabs at times, but what can we do. We have no choice." The witness also told us about one company commander who briefed his soldiers and explained to them how to take apart the rubber ammo tampons and fire them at people's heads in order to at least try to hit the eye of a demonstrator, and how guys in the company used to laugh about this later.

One of the things he said at the time sounded to us like a wild exaggeration. He claimed that the sergeant major bragged about a conversation he had with the battalion commander, who claimed that the chief of staff issued an order to start killing, lifting any limitations in the designated area. No more inhibitions. "Six Palestinian corpses a day" are a must, never mind where. We did not take this testimony seriously: the sergeant major, so we thought, just wanted to boast of his proximity to the highest echelons and important goings-on.

Eventually I read *Boomerang*, a book written by reporters Ofer Shelah and Raviv Drucker, which had a whole chapter about "Mofaz' Tanzim" (the chief of staff's gang), a commonly used appellation in the army at the time. It described the reckless, "trigger happy" field commanders who acted in the spirit of the supreme commander of the armed forces. The book relates how in this highest capacity, Shaul Mofaz told commanders that he expected a daily quota of Palestinian casualties: ten a day in every designated area of a regional brigade. Only then did I realize that the sergeant major was not being vain, nor did our witness exaggerate . . .

How could I have commanded soldiers on behalf of Shaul Mofaz?

How could I overlook the truth, overlook reality?

How did they manage to brainwash me with the myth of the most moral army in the world?

Few Israelis know anything about their own army's rules of engagement. Fewer still oppose them. But whoever learns about them and dares to put two and two together will reach an inevitable conclusion: procedures have executors, and for every person killed, there is a killer. That killer might very well be the youth movement counselor you admired, or your neighbor's delicate son, or the intimidated boy from your grade-school class. Perhaps even your own boyfriend—imagine that!

From the day I was assigned, along with my fellow officer training cadets, to the Gaza Strip in October 2000 until the time of this writing, I managed to: be a commander, become a civilian, get a bit confused, go on a post-army trip, study for my bachelor's degree, and do my post-graduation tour. During this period of time, our IDF managed to kill over two thousand Palestinians who took no part in any combat action whatsoever. (And at the time the above was translated for you, my English reader, that number had increased to 3,088 Palestinians.)

CHAPTER 31

Another testimony I took, which was personally significant, was given by a military medic. I had befriended him when, together, we led a day trip for new immigrant youngsters who had lost their siblings in the terrorist bombing at the Dolphinarium Club in Tel Aviv. For most of his military service the medic was assigned to areas other than the Occupied Territories. But on one of the rare occasions when he was assigned there, he witnessed a military doctor who, having established the death of a Palestinian, summoned several other medics to gather around the body.

"It was weird. On radio they announced that 'the scum went stiff' and called in all the medics. The doctor used this opportunity to give us a field anatomy lesson. He took out a scalpel, made incisions in the skin and showed us the various skin layers. He reviewed the procedures for treating a burn, and took out the liver and showed us how it connected to the digestive tract and blood circulatory system."

I actually remember his gestures, as if he were cutting into his own skin, extracting his own liver.

This doctor showed them more organs in the dead body and gave professional explanations about medical care. One of the medics could not bear this and left at the very beginning, throwing up. Our witness, too, left before the lesson ended.

"Why did you leave in the middle?" I asked.

"I don't know. I thought a dissection demonstration in the middle of the street was plain sick."

"Did anyone say anything to you? Was anyone annoyed at you for not staying?"

"Not really. You know, this was no basic training maneuver. We were in the midst of a military operation. It was considered a kind of treat. Everyone was really excited about it."

At Breaking the Silence lectures and encounters, I refrained from citing such testimonies. I spoke mostly about my own experiences and those of my subordinates: about occupying the home near Tul Karm, about "shows of force and presence," about curfew enforcement, about destructive everyday routines—how destructive those routines were for our minds. For that was the central topic of our lectures: a verbal and visual illustration of the banal truth, by now a cliché, that "occupation corrupts."

The doctor episode and other repulsive testimonies I used to save for the question-and-answer period following my lecture. One of the usual reactions to the lectures was a kind of relieved, self-righteous sigh: "If this is what you need to break the silence about, then we are still okay." The harsher testimonies were a fitting answer to such a remark. Sadly, my arsenal contained quite a few such testimonies.

At first, some of the reporters we approached refused to publish the "anatomy lesson" testimony. After the army denied it, the media preferred to let it go. But it was eventually published, albeit reservedly, on *Haaretz's* front page, which was quite an achievement. Satisfaction, however, soon turned into a deep sense of failure, because even this horrendous event had no resonance; it generated no public demand to conduct further inquiries. My faith in the willingness of my people to know and change reality was shaken even more, and along with it, my own sense of belonging.

CHAPTER 32

I recall another testimony, entirely different than the rest, given by a young man who had served in the years between the two Intifadas, during the Oslo period (mid- to late 1990s). He served in what was known as the District Coordination Office (DCO), a mechanism set up for liaison and security cooperation between the Israeli and Palestinian authorities in the Occupied Territories.

"Intifada": the word entered the Hebrew language defined more or less as "terrorist warfare." Do any of us even know the original meaning of this word? It means "tremor." For my part, you should understand that I was not fighting against any "tremor" or "uprising." I was fighting "terror."

So the fellow had dealt quite often with matters that he was supposed to keep silent about—matters of intelligence and collaborator recruitment. At the beginning of our conversation, when I explained the purpose of our testimony-gathering and the standards of journalist confidentiality we abided by, we agreed that he would not touch upon those matters during the interview. We are not interested in them, I said. We had no legal way of revealing them and would not want to get him in trouble for violating laws regarding "state security."

"State security"—what the hell is that? And where does this term get its immense power? Perhaps from the fact that it is so automatically familiar? "State security" is in fact no less automatic than such terms as "security forces," "moral occupation," "defense forces" and "Jewish and democratic."

So, little girl, if I describe to you in further detail the talk I had with the witness from the DCO, I might violate laws regarding "state security." So I shall not do it. For I—you must have already understood this from my previous stories—am not especially fond of taking risks. I am not one to rush ahead and get beaten up at a demonstration, not one to march, head held high, off to military or any other kind of jail. I decided long ago not to violate any law. If the law becomes unbearable, then I will exchange my old dream of a little house in my home village of Kfar Yehezkel for a new dream of a little house abroad with the same beloved wife and four imaginary children. Some would say this is cowardice, but as far as I am concerned, it is a simple order of priorities: laws are geographic. Man isn't. A human being is not a tree—certainly not I, not the person I've became since losing my Holocaust. At this phase of my life, I still owe a heavy debt to Israeli society and to Palestinian society. I was among the brainwashed who committed crimes in the Occupied Territories, and the quiet struggle over public opinion that Breaking the Silence is conducting is also a kind of penance for me. But I have no intention of foregoing all my precious years on this earth for the sake of these struggles.

And still, perhaps "cowardice" is the concise, precise definition for a life philosophy of this sort?

Anyway, I am willing to say here only one thing that I learned from that witness about recruiting collaborators—I would not want to be a Palestinian marked as suitable for collaboration. For there is no turning back. If you refuse, you're lost. And if you agree, you're just as lost. Your must choose between being pursued by us or being pursued by them for the rest of your life.

What the witness did tell on record was the story of a certain complaint lodged by some Palestinian, perhaps for the violation of an agreement or for "damage to a Palestinian person." The witness described how, from the moment it was filed, the complaint was passed around aimlessly, until it was thrown into the trash bin next to his superior officer's desk. This was another chronicle of a small absurdity, one more minor cause among the many causes of the great explosion of October 2000—the Second Intifada—which caught me during my officer training and eventually brought about the theft of my Holocaust, as it shed much blood on both the weak side and the weaker side of this conflict.

CHAPTER 33

The harshest testimonies have not yet been published, and many of them probably never will be. The fictitious witness who meant to incriminate us caused us to set strict and clear criteria for publishing a "heavy" episode: we would not publicize such a story unless we possessed two mutually independent testimonies of the same incident. This decision has frustrated us very often, but at times it has also given us additional motivation and generated unexpected thrills as we looked for further evidence to support one story or another.

At times we felt like actors in detective dramas. We gave some of these dramas titles, such as "G.'s Feats," "The Yossi Bachar Horror Show," "M. the Doctor" (which I already told you), "Revenge," and also "The Hot Tape"—which I'll tell you now.

"The Hot Tape," or as it was more commonly known, "Whitewasher S.," began as most of these dramas do: a chance meeting with a soldier willing to talk.

"Are you looking at something, man?"

We're sitting on the lawn on campus.

"We've met before, haven't we? At Pablo's? You were with Tali, remember? Why are you saying you don't remember?"

"Where do I know you from?"

"Maybe from recon squad commanders' training?

"What can I do . . ."

"Why, where did you serve?"

"Nahal. And you?"

"Paratroopers, man—respect—but didn't finish there. I stayed on as a special means officer in the unit."

"Really."

Then we meet at a mutual friend's place and get better acquainted. A beer, snacks, small talk: scholarships, student union jobs, cooking skills that improve as distance from mom's kitchen becomes a living fact. I say something about Breaking the Silence. He is reserved about our extremism or our one-sidedness, but identifies with the feelings themselves and with our motive. Finally he agrees to talk.

The recording session in his room begins as a pleasant conversation and continues cautiously and noncommittally as he lays out the first story he has prepared. His testimony opens with a description of the goings-on in Hebron in the first month of the Second Intifada, as seen through the eyes of a soldier stationed at an army post: heavy weapons are fired, power gives pleasure, guys shoot at a lamp, miss and hit a car, it blows up just like in an American movie. There is surveillance in the area; the cameras catch the guys blowing up the car and every-one cracks up laughing. The company commander—let's call him S.—is terribly excited, however. He wants more cars

213

blown up. Cars are targeted but they only get holes in them. No more explode.

An ambulance is shot, homes are shot. Soldiers shoot wildly into residential areas without even knowing where the shots they're supposedly reacting to are coming from. They're not even sure it's really enemy fire. Neighborhoods are sprayed with gunfire and the guys laugh their hearts out.

The witness and I take a break from recording and go out for a cigarette on the porch in the nice Jerusalem chill. Exams are coming up in two weeks and we're wasting an evening . . . He wonders whether to continue his present studies or switch over to chemical or electrical engineering.

Down in the street, brakes screech at a stop light—an accident? No. Everything seems alright.

"More coffee? Tali baked cookies. You should have a taste."

"Is this recording?"

"Just a second . . . Yes. Go ahead."

"Where was I?"

"Hebron, man. Searches."

"Oh."

He describes his first entries into homes. He proceeds with descriptions of operations in the West Bank that became looting sprees: video cameras, digital cameras, CD players, money, jewelry, cell phones, food and beverages, souvenirs of all types—systemic theft at gunpoint, in state uniform. He keeps "that cell phone there on the shelf, a reminder of that which must not be done." He was a religious fellow back then, observed the Sabbath. Nowadays he would never steal like that. He regrets it. He explains that everyone did this . . . and . . .

So far nothing new. Another testimony about loose reins in an exhausted paratrooper company. But then comes "the worst story I witnessed in the army."

As an interviewer I already know that nearly every witness has one story that really weighs on his heart. So here is our witness's worst story. It is also the first of a series of stories about Commander S.'s "hot tape."

They are standing guard in a two-story post. The guys above are supposed to look out over the surrounding streets while those below are supposed to shoot when necessary. When a masked person is detected or a blast heard in the area, live fire is used—shoot to kill. But if children are throwing stones, they must be dispersed by rubber ammunition, stun and teargas grenades. The guys above are not supposed to shoot. Why? Because a bullet from above would hit a head, and the point here is to keep children off the street, not to make them drop dead in it.

Noontime. The kids are throwing stones as usual. The fellows below at the post fire teargas and stun grenades and rubber ammo. The guys above want their share too, and demand some crowd-dispersal fun for themselves as well. They are the senior ranking soldiers in the company and deserve respect. If they ask for something, they must be obliged. The soldiers below hand them the rubber ammo shooting fixture. After several shots from above, instead of the flat sound of the cartridge, the sharp crack of live rounds is heard. And again. And again. And then silence all around.

"Just a moment, man. Explain this for the recording. Not everyone knows what this cartridge does."

"Sure. The cartridge has no bullet. It only blasts off the tampon to make the rubber ammunition cluster scatter apart."

So suddenly live ammunition is fired from above. Someone breaks into the radio net on brigade frequency, screaming: "Why are you firing live? Who opened live fire in this area? Who's shooting, damn it?!"

A DCO officer is heard on the communication system: "A local is down in the market." (A Palestinian has been killed in the market). The officer arrives running, and asks—or to be more precise, goes ballistic: "Who opened fire?! Who?!"

And our witness answers him: "We didn't shoot." "I don't know." "I didn't hear anything."

"Look," our witness explains to the tiny microphone attached to his lapel. "These are senior soldiers . . . You can't tell them anything . . ."

Then S. arrives, the company's terrible commander, fuming and spewing and scolding his men. "Who opened live fire here?" Our friend answers once again: he heard nothing, saw nothing, knows nothing. But this company commander, the same one who craved burning vehicles and had no contempt for looters in his own company, now flies into a rage. He must have realized he could get in deep trouble. He goes upstairs to the senior guys and accuses them, demands answers. But no one admits that live fire was shot from the post. A minute goes by, and another, and again the radio screeches: at the company's intelligence post, a lookout monitor, like the ones who

216

filmed the burning car, says the commander better hurry down to see something on tape. The great commander gets into his Jeep, slams the door and nervously gestures where to drive. A minute later the Jeep halts, brakes screaming, below the intelligence post. Something is going on at the post. The witness and the soldiers who are with him have no idea what it is. The soldier who fired from the top post did not admit a thing. Still, he was penalized, perhaps for killing a young vendor — about the same age as the soldiers — as he was unloading his goods in the market. The vendor was hit in the back and killed. The punishment: thirty-five days of maintenance chores at the battalion base, which usually means gardening and kitchen duty. This is harsh punishment for an older combatant. Punishment does not fall lightly upon the more experienced soldiers.

But the issue here is not the light punishment. We have already heard about the officer who was fined one hundred shekels after his marksman took down a local kid. The fascinating question here is not the penalty for killing a chance Palestinian in the market, but what happened at the surveillance post.

So let's sort out what we know here: we have accounts of looting and indiscriminate shooting, and a strange punishment given to a senior soldier for opening live fire from his post. We know someone was killed in the market at the exact time when live fire was opened from the post. We also know that the whole affair was silenced at company level — no inquiry, nothing mentioned to others. We also have a testimony about hearsay in the company: "There is talk in the company that S. received a video recording of the shooting and killing of the guy in the market"; "People say the guy was killed by a bullet in the back"; "People say the video disappeared"; "There are whispers that a guy was grounded because of this"; "Apparently no one knows about this at battalion headquarters."

We found no corroborating evidence. We asked the witness to call friends—perhaps he'd find someone willing to talk. The witness flatly refused. He wouldn't risk exposing himself as a squealer. The path was blocked. We tried to locate intelligence personnel present at the time but found no one. We did find surveillance operators. They knew nothing of the event but were willing to lend a hand. They called friends of theirs who had been in Hebron at the time, and secretly recorded those phone calls. "Yes, that was one hell of a fucked-up story there," one of the men answered, and said no more. In those conversations, time and again men avoided the question we wished to ask. Obviously, something significant had taken place. But what exactly was on that tape, what the great commander S. had concealed—that we could not uncover.

We thought the material looked reliable enough and decided to publicize it as it was. The reporter we approached was convinced that the first part of the story was true enough: live fire had been opened from the post and it accidentally killed the vendor in the market. As for the second part— namely, that the incident had been videotaped, that the company commander buried the tape and concealed evidence, that the shooter received absurd punishment, in short: that S.

had whitewashed things big-time—no certainty could be established. The press story nonetheless raised suspicion of whitewashing and provoked a demand for further investigation by the Military Police. The second half of the story, then, was doomed to remain in our archives, in the file for uncorroborated stories.

A year went by, and another. Yehuda Shaul was leading a tour of Hebron, as he did every Friday morning: this time, not for diplomats, nor for Israeli parliamentarians, nor for supreme-court judges from abroad, not even for Jewish community leaders or rabbis. This was just a regular tour for the general public through the Jews-only streets of Hebron, the City of the Patriarchs, ours and theirs as well. He stood in front of the checkpoint named "The Policeman's Post." Someone in the audience asked whether this was the spot where a soldier had urinated from the roof of a Palestinian home on a girl playing in her own yard, as had recently been reported on the news.

"No, we'll get there shortly."

At that spot Yehuda usually tells about the first time he had to open live fire in Hebron. He says he was stunned at the briefing he had received: hurling live grenades inside a town? It didn't make any sense. A grenade is a destructive and imprecise weapon. After all, in our firing maneuvers with grenade launchers in the Negev desert, we are required to maintain a huge safe distance from army bases, other forces in training, residential areas, and even nature reserves. There, in the Negev sands, you launch a grenade at the range of a kilometer and a half and watch the dust rising from the blast, then correct a little bit to the right, another cloud of dust, a bit to the left, bull's eye. A good grenade-launcher operator will hit the target with his third grenade. No one would scold you for succeeding only on your fifth try. But in a town? No way can I launch grenades with an imprecise weapon in an urban neighborhood, thought Yehuda as he received that briefing at 13:00. At 18:00 that day he obeyed orders and fired at that neighborhood just as everyone else did.

Just as I did, too, firing a heavy machine gun on the outskirts of Al Khader village. We were ordered to open fire and, unthinking, I did. I looked at my men and saw them spraying bullets from their rifles and the platoon machine gun at the quarry between the Jewish settlement in which we were situated and the Arab neighborhoods. I watched them, saw they were delighted: it was their first "operational" fire. I looked at them and saw myself as well, realized I was enjoying shooting. I knew we had no idea whom or what we were shooting at. I ordered them to hold their fire. Someone detected movement in the quarry and asked permission to open fire. Right behind me stood a reserves tank company commander. He was the commander in charge of the post and I had arrived there with rookies as reinforcements. I passed the question over to him: Open fire?

"As you see fit," he answered.

"Is he armed?" one of the reservists asked.

"I think so," one of my men yelled.

"Nothing on him," someone from inside the tank retorted.

"I'm losing sight of him. May I fire?" my marksman asked.

"No," I answered.

I saw firemen trying to put out fires inside the village. The tank next to me had fired illumination bombs but had no idea how to aim them. "It's not what we had when we were regulars," the man yelled from his tank. The bombs burst into flames on houses, not in the air. They started fires. "Why weren't we taught about this in pre-combat practice?"

I looked around for ambulances. There weren't any. That calmed me a bit—it must mean there are no casualties. I got down from the post and turned on the radio, wanted to hear that no one had been killed because God only knows where we shot: we had orders to open fire and so we did. "Palestinian fire was opened from the Al Khader area south of Bethlehem. Our forces returned fire towards the sources of the shooting. No casualties reported."

"Sources of the shooting." Heard that? Even the shooter himself did not hear the lie at the time.

I consider the decision I made not to shoot the man in the quarry to be the most important decision I've ever made.

On that Hebron tour, Yehuda Shaul made an exception to the rule and did not tell the story of the grenade-launcher. He chose, instead, to talk about how the vendor, called Mansour Taha Ahmad, was shot to death in the market by soldiers at the army post, and about the punishment received by the shooter. If anyone killed me, I'd rather have him go scot-free than pay for taking my life with thirty-five days of community gardening work. Yehuda said nothing about the whitewashing affair, for he is a cautious, meticulous chap, but as fate would have it, just that once Yehuda decided to do things differently and talked about that shooting. Among his listeners was a young man who got up and said: "Man, do you know what really happened there? I do." The fellow was a former intelligence staff member who had just returned from a trip to India with his good friend, and his good friend had told him a story.

Anyone who has ever gone through basic training is familiar with the yell "Contact!," which is usually accompanied by a tap on the shoulder. Sometimes the tap is more like a powerful blow and the yell more like a roar. This is what a soldier laying in ambush yells when he detects the enemy. Its immediate meaning is: find shelter and open fire. It is also used to test the alertness of a trainee's speed and power during shooting practice.

With or without the tap on the shoulder, it is the order to open fire at the shooting range. When the trainees hear "Contact!" they assume a certain firing position, depending on the instructions they are given beforehand: they either prostrate themselves on the ground, kneel, or stand and hold their rifle-butt to the outer tip of their collar bone. *Rat-tat-tat* at the center of the target, then they snap on the safety catch and relax until the next time they hear "Contact!"

And this is what the intelligence man's friend had told him, and he told us on the tour that day:

"We were sitting at our post in Hebron, looking out over the street and part of the market. Suddenly, we heard shots in the street. We looked to see who was shooting and where, and realized the shots were coming from the post on the roof. The soldier was shooting towards the market. We pointed the camera at him and recorded. The soldier stood on the roof, far from the railing. Suddenly, his pal hit him on the shoulder, as is done in shooting practice. The soldier took three running steps towards the railing, got into shooting pose and fired: *Rat-tat-tat-tat*. He lowered his weapon and got back. Another blow on the shoulder, run, shelter, *rat-tat-tat-tat*. Safety catch, lower weapon. They were playing shooting range, roof-top roulette. One would alert the other and the other would shoot. Again, alert, once again, gunfire. Aiming at the market. Several times. Not even looking at what happens down below. They're playing around, man. Do you get it? *Rat-tat-tat-tat*.

"We didn't know what to do. My commander hesitated. Neither he nor we wanted to squeal on soldiers and harm them. They're our buddies. We decided to show the tape to their company commander, let him decide."

CHAPTER 34

"Hi, this is Eitan of the Ministry of Defense speaking." The voice was assertive, his tone authoritative.

That was the beginning of my first phone conversation with Eitan.

"What is it?" I asked, trying to sound as cool and masculine as any Israeli male.

I imagined this was another investigator wanting to pose some questions following a publication in the media of a testimony by Breaking the Silence. Such questions, I knew, focus on us, not on the actual incident.

With the same authoritative tone that only "Eitan of the Ministry of Defense" knew how to use, he asked, "Say, were you in Company F of Battalion 932 from X until Y?"

"I think so," I said. "But I'm studying with friends for an exam right now. Can't talk. Call me tonight."

"I'm only here until five. I'll call tomorrow."

"Tomorrow is no good. I'm at work all day," I lied. "If you want precise answers with certain dates and . . . I have to go check in my picture albums, or talk to my buddies. Call me the day after tomorrow."

"Okay, we'll talk." And he hung up.

I quickly figured out where I was at the time he mentioned and could have answered him that very day, but I wanted to tape my conversation with him and didn't have a recorder for my landline at home. At the first meetings in Breaking the Silence, after the planted witness affair and other strange events, we used to take out our cell phone batteries while speaking with each other, to make sure we were not being tapped. "The fact that you're paranoid does not mean you're not being followed," we used to make fun of ourselves. When people like Eitan call us, it always pays to be ready.

My days were filled with work and study and I couldn't get a recorder, so when he called two days later, I didn't answer. I called him back at ten past five, just to make sure he wouldn't answer. More days went by, another call and another apology: "I'm in class," another postponement.

The date Eitan was interested in fell precisely between my two assignments: I had left my platoon in the company about which he inquired, and was posted as deputy commander of another company. The next time he called me, I was driving. I had just finished a rest break at Golani Junction on my way north to prepare a guided tour of the Galilee. It was one of those moments when you are caught holding a sandwich in one hand, a cell phone in another, and with the third and fourth you try to get out of a parking lot with a honking bus behind you whose driver is furious with you for having blocked him. I didn't notice it was Eitan on the phone and had already answered. What could I do? I couldn't go on avoiding him and even my girlfriend was sure I was just being paranoid: all he wanted was to ask me a question. Why record him in the first place?

What a mistake! If only I had a recording of that phone call now, I could enjoy the pleasure of seeing Eitan's spokesman twist and cringe as he attempted to explain Eitan's behavior. He asked me if I was at Qalandiya Checkpoint that day. I asked him why he was interested in what happened at Qalandiya two and a half years ago, and to my amazement I received a detailed answer.

"We have some local complaining that a soldier of yours at the checkpoint made him drink urine, and he's suing for damages." "Suing?" I asked. There's an Israeli law preventing Palestinians from suing the army. The State does not pay reparations to victims of the Intifada, right? But Eitan answered that in this case the law was not that easy to enforce. At that point in the conversation I still thought this Eitan was trying to get down to the truth, and I wanted to help him.

"Listen, Eitan," I said. "Let me make a few phone calls to some friends from the company. If this really took place, I'll get the story for you. I just wasn't with them any longer by that time, but I'm willing to help you out here."

"No," he answered. "I'm looking for someone, preferably an officer, who will testify that your unit was no longer there that day, that you had already been replaced. Say that by that time some reserves unit was already manning the area. This way we can counter his testimony, because the local insists that they were the same soldiers who had been stationed there for weeks earlier and that he can identify faces."

Son of a bitch!!! I cursed him silently. And my maker as well, for not recording these words.

"If that is your case," I said, "I really can't help you, especially since we were certainly there at the time. You can also check the operations logs."

He ruined my trip that day. I was so annoyed with him and with myself! Damn—how could I not have recorded that conversation! How I wished I could have made that story public! But what could I do with no evidence? Perhaps I should have sought out the lawyer representing that Palestinian and testified on his behalf that Eitan tried to whitewash this case. I didn't think of it then.

If only I had the chance to talk to you again, Eitan, you who walk into your air-conditioned office every morning and don't answer the phone after five p.m.

Tell me, Eitan, what do you say to your buddies about what you do at work? Protecting our state's economic interests? How, in your opinion, is it possible that the State of Israel—by law—does not compensate people, innocent civilians, who were hurt by its apparatuses? A state that owes its initial economic growth to the reparations that flowed to it justly: but that shouldn't be written at all, for Holocaust is Holocaust and don't you dare compare if you want anyone to read what you write . . .

Okay, I'm not comparing, only . . .

That's right, neither can we sue Hamas or Islamic Jihad for the damages that their suicide bombings wrought upon Israeli cities. Good answer, Eitan. When you're right, you're right.

But listen, I'm still annoyed that you compare our actions to their terrorist attacks. What business have terrorist organizations in a court of law? Yes, you do compare! And do you realize what you do to us, Eitan? You place us, our State, me, on the list of organizations that are not liable to be sued because they are not legally responsible for their actions. Not even for "exceptional deeds" by "rotten apples" acting in our name.

But forgive me, Eitan, why am I pestering you? The law was passed by the Knesset, Israel's legislature. And what are you? You are merely a minor official of the executive branch, a cog that enforces the law and tries to spare a pittance for the state treasury. And, surely, you are obeying orders.

CHAPTER 35

The first time I traveled to Qalandiya Checkpoint as a civilian was for a very modest interview. British students were filming a documentary as their final study project. Yehuda suggested they interview me at the checkpoint. I didn't want to go back there.

I was afraid of Palestinians and, even more, of my own feelings. For I actually had unpleasant bodily sensations whenever I traveled to the Occupied Territories as a civilian at the time: a strange malaise of sorts, slight nausea and even an unfamiliar sense of self-revulsion that made me want to wash up urgently. But even the cold, refreshing shower at home would not help. It did not relieve me of this irrational sense of filth.

Yehuda picked me up on his motorcycle, the "service van" of Breaking the Silence, and we drove from Jerusalem to the checkpoint. On the way he tried to calm me down. The problem was that his very presence—beard and skullcap and everything they represent in the Occupied Territories— only intensified my fears. I was hoping that at the checkpoint itself, the British students, with their foreignness and cameras, would temper my Israeli-ness somewhat and thus shield and reassure me.

But although I had implored them to get there before we did, they were late and had not yet arrived when we pulled up. They did not realize the complexity of this place—in general and for me in particular. When they finally arrived, we mounted the small hill overlooking the checkpoint. There they interviewed and filmed me against the background of the area where I and my subordinates fired teargas and cleared away vendors and taxis.

A person who has never seen a major checkpoint such as Qalandiya or Huwwara cannot begin to imagine how it affects everyday life in the entire region. Since vehicles are hardly ever allowed through, both sides of the barrier are soon filled with improvised bus and cab stations. A bustling business develops there, of porters who carry pedestrians' luggage and personal belongings or goods in small handcarts, backpacks and plastic bags. And since people are forced to wait for hours in long lines, small outdoor markets develop: venders offering food and drink, cold *tamarhindi*—date juice—or plain tap water in plastic cups. Other people improvise stalls selling cloth, clothes, hats, shoes, school gear; and both adults and children improvise small canteens, brewing coffee and tea.

Sometimes I try to visualize what my own life would be like if every time I went out I ran into the "chance stoplight." This is an imaginary machine I devised especially for this exercise: it would determine at random the duration of my wait— between twenty minutes and five hours. The "chance stoplight" does not harass or humiliate, it only replicates the technical aspect of the checkpoint. I replay the previous day in my mind, and try to determine what I would readily give up. I imagine the coming week and decide I would not help Yossi move to his new place by making a few trips with my father's old truck. I decide to go shopping only once and warn myself not to forget anything. I deliberate over whether to go out on a date or spend an evening with friends, and I have a hard time giving up my habit of going out every evening just to get some air.

When I arrived for my interview with the British students, I was surprised by the number of stalls. When my own company was assigned to the checkpoint and I was its commander for eight hours out of every twenty-four, we didn't let the venders get so close. One of the company's recon Jeeps was tasked with chasing them off. We wrote cardboard signs in Arabic instructing the venders to get the hell out. They immediately removed the signs. We often hurled teargas and stun grenades at them. Whenever a taxi driver insisted on waiting too close to the checkpoint—hoping he would be the lucky one to get passengers—we would hurl a teargas grenade into the cab through the window, just to make certain that this driver would not earn anything in the next few hours and would learn his lesson and never come so close again.

In the interview I told them how I felt as a checkpoint commander, how fatigue aggregated with fear to become apathy as the days rolled by, how human compassion and judgment are gradually lost. I described the mental process that a soldier at the checkpoint undergoes, how at first he tries to be nice, to smile, explain, keep calm. How, eventually, he turns into an automaton, and how at the end of this process he no longer sees the Palestinians as human beings.

During my army service I thought I believed all humans were equal, that everyone had the right to live in dignity and freedom. I believed that this situation I was in was temporary and imposed upon us in order to cope with terrorism. Now, as my memory—film-like—replays the events that transpired when I was in charge at Qalandiya Checkpoint, I know this was all a lie, a denial mechanism and a distortion of reality, a mechanism that enabled me to function without contradicting my own set of values, which in turn were being warped. Now I know that had I seen the crowds in front of me as human beings just like me, I would see how they were harassed even before carrying out my assignments: in the endless waiting forced upon them, standing in the baking sun behind high fences, in horribly crowded conditions, in an unbearable cacophony of shouts, quarrels, crying babies, pleading women and elderly people, screaming venders and the stench concocted by massive crowding and heat.

I told the British students about one of the events from this memory-film of mine. The memory of this event struck me at one of the Breaking the Silence meetings as clear proof that in the crowds passing me day-in-day-out, I did not see humans— or at least not humans equal to myself or the people now sitting around me at a charming "mochillero" café in Kochin, a city on the shores of the Arabian Sea.

It was a particularly hot day. The line was long and crowded as usual: men, women, children and babies, porters with their bundles — all pressed and crushed against one another by the mass behind them. The soldiers, as on any crowded day there, pushed back the people standing at the head of the line, and occasionally even closed the checkpoint completely, a punitive measure for disorderly behavior. At times the soldiers do it out of anger, at other times out of real fear, when the minimum necessary distance is not maintained between them and the crowd.

But the frequent closure of the checkpoint only intensifies the crowding and shoving and the crush of the masses in back who cannot see what is happening at the front of the line, close to the soldiers' posts. And I was in charge of this entire enterprise and its two production lines: several entry checking posts for those traveling to Ar-Ram, and an exit checking post for the Ramallah-bound. The raw material: about 2,500 disgruntled Palestinians a day.

Through our communications system I was updated about the current orders and passed them on to all the soldiers at the checkpoint. At times I helped out checking trucks, and here and there I was called upon to solve problems that came up at the checking and guard posts. I also passed on Palestinians' ID numbers to headquarters, which passed them on to the higher HQ and on to the General Security Services (Shabak) or to the female soldier handling its "wanted" name-lists, and then back down the same chain of command, from the regional command to the brigade, battalion, company and checkpoint. When all the rungs of this bureaucratic ladder worked flawlessly, when none of the office personnel happened to be dozing off or in the bathroom, when nobody forgot or made a mistake while passing on the name or number of someone wishing to cross the checkpoint, then that Palestinian was fortunate enough to be sent on his way within half an hour or an hour.

At this point I should explain the idea of "delaying." It differs from "drying out," for example. A person "delayed" is a random passerby at the checkpoint who is required to wait while the wheels of military bureaucracy turn and search for "security information" about him. His ID is taken from him and he is usually required to wait, sitting on the ground by the checkpoint. "Drying out" a Palestinian, in contrast, means that he stands, hands shackled behind his back in tight plastic cuffs, feet sometimes shackled as well, blindfolded with a piece of "flannel"—a strip of cloth used to polish gun barrels—and usually kept out of sight behind a concrete block or small shack. Unlike the "delayed," the Palestinian being "dried out" is not waiting for anything—except, perhaps, a show of kindness on the part of the checkpoint commander, who may decide to slightly relieve the pressure of the plastic cuffs on his wrists, or allow him to have a sip of water.

"Drying out" is a punitive measure—to punish a Palestinian who has complained, yelled, cursed, bypassed the line, or been rude to a soldier. But not only that: it could also be because he has an annoying moustache—dry him out. His shirt is ugly—dry him out. Your buddy has been killed in a terrorist attack—dry him out. Dry out whom? Anyone you please. How long? As long as you please. An hour. Eight hours. Why? Just because.

It had been especially hot on that day, I told the British students. The line, as usual, was long and crowded. I was standing by the checking posts, making sure everything was operating smoothly. I looked at the line and noticed a young blond woman in western summer clothes standing pressed in between sweating men and the high fence. I approached her and signaled to her to get out of the line and bypass it. I would check her passport and let her proceed, I thought. She made some room between herself and the others around her, waved her finger at me and yelled in foreign-accented English: "What's the difference between me and the rest of the people here?"

I didn't say anything but she repeated the same words again and again, and got more and more flushed. "Tell me what the difference is! Why shouldn't they come around with me?" I smiled and answered her quietly, calmly and politely, that if she wanted to stand in line, suit herself. *"Tfadhali,* you may wait." I saw how the men around her attempted to leave her some elbow room, and noticed especially two of them who were trying hard not to crush her.

I recalled this detail again when I traveled with my girl-friend in Jordan. When we rode a public bus, men always took care not to touch her, and likewise at markets and bustling streets—room was always made for her with that typically demonstrative Arab gesture. Later, when we traveled on from Jordan to India, we noticed the sharp contrast: here people were always bumping into you, whether you were a man or a woman. They would always touch you and never apologize. But in my Qalandiya Checkpoint days I was not busy analyzing cultural differences. I was supervising the smooth operations of soldiers on duty to prevent terrorist attacks.

And on that especially hot day, after saluting her noble stance with my affected politeness, and letting her go on and get crushed in line, I silently answered her question to myself:

1. The checkpoint is meant to prevent terrorist attacks and arrest suspects.
2. She is not a suspect.
3. She is on her way to Ramallah, not to Jerusalem.
4. I have no idea what she does in Ramallah, nor am I really interested.
5. She is not a potential terrorist.

Hence, there was no reason for her to suffer along with everyone else in that crowded line. In spite of my reasoning, which I bothered to iterate in my mind as if I were standing trial for racism, I admired her. I was touched by her willingness to make sacrifices for the dignity of those standing around her. For a rare moment she made me feel very bad about what I was doing. But soon enough I repeated my imaginary response to her.

Today my eyes are open, my denial mechanisms have collapsed, my false security arguments have evaporated, and I know the answer she was seeking from me, an answer that even now brings on tears and chokes me up, although by now I have said this so many times.

I saw a beautiful blond woman whose delicate looks reminded me slightly of my older sister, and I felt sorry for her. For her and not for all those young women and girls and students and older women, rich and poor, crushed there in front of me, day in day out on my eight-hour-long shifts. I saw her pushed and sweating among all the rest and she did not look to me like all the rest. She was different from the "locals." Different from those subjected to military law. She was like me. And I was the law.

The security lie I had repeated mantra-like for myself and for my soldiers— *to prevent a terrorist attack, to prevent a terrorist attack, to prevent a . . .* —could not rescue me from the young European woman's verdict. That crowded line was between Ar-Ram and Ramallah, and whoever wished to attack Ramallah—was always welcome! We all knew that at a short distance east of the checkpoint was a wide hole in the barbed wire fences. I took the British students there and the hole was still in the fence, two years after I had left the area. They could film it, as well as the people who scampered through it. That hole was proof for me that the security argument explaining the huge checkpoint of Qalandiya was a lie and that the true reason for the existence of that checkpoint was to harass the population, weaken it and make it easier to control. It is those who obey the rules whom the checkpoint harasses the most.

Having concluded the interview, we walked around, filming the line of people waiting to cross the checkpoint so the film

237

editors would later be able to voice their narration against the background of people crowded inside. Then Yehuda did something I did not understand, and at first even tried to resist. He forced me deep into that crowded waiting line and said something like: "I did this myself in Hebron. It's good for you, stand in line!" I tried to turn around and get out, but he gently gripped my shoulder and pushed me back inside. I stopped resisting.

I don't know whether the shudder I sense now as I write and tell you these things comes from too much nicotine or from the force of this recollection—a bit of both, I guess.

It was already noon. I felt as though I was watching a complex thriller from the middle and not understanding the plot, but it was shaking my every nerve ending, touching every bit of my skin. At times the film would go mute. I saw a vendor selling sunglasses call out to me but did not hear what he said. Suddenly, the sound was back and I realized he had called out to me a few times. I refused him with a nod, not uttering a word, so as not to identify myself and break the silence I was in.

With that same mute nod I refused the child who offered me coffee in a small plastic cup. I shuffled further along the queue. Through the wire fence I saw soldiers get out of a staff Jeep at the same spot where two years earlier I had gotten out of such a Jeep. It was a changing of the guard at the checkpoint. I looked at the soldiers from the new shift approach their pals at the observation and checking posts and exchange words with them.

Great, I thought. Now they are carrying out a procedure we always had trouble implementing: any soldier leaving a post is required to update his replacement about new instructions, the wanted list and the general situation at the checkpoint. He must show him all the "delayed" and "dried out" individuals and hand him their IDs so that the new fellow can eventually release them. But when a soldier concludes his eight-hour shift of stressful, strained activity—both physical and emotional—all he wants is to get out of there as quickly as possible. He wants to throw everything away, fill his stomach with some army chow, make contact with someone he's close to in the outside world and stretch out on his bed, into a world of his own thoughts and dreams and some peace and quiet . . . Got to hand it to the commanders of this company, I thought—their soldiers take the trouble to go through the replacement procedure despite the grinding routine of eight-hours-duty-eight-hours-all-the-rest.

Suddenly, I was terribly startled. Looking at the Palestinians crowded around me, I felt they could hear my thoughts and figure out that I was in fact a soldier like the ones across the fence. I was also afraid of the soldiers. What if that idiot over there had not unloaded the machine-gun pointed at us, or if that other jerk went crazy and opened fire? I was really scared. I moved a few steps to the right and back and thus lost my place in line to some boys who crowded ahead of me. But now at least I was out of the soldiers' sight.

Then my turn came. I wasn't ready for this. I hadn't thought at all about what I would say. I was standing in front of that concrete

239

cube, facing a female soldier, her helmet a bit loose, her lips dry and sun-burnt, and she was yelling "Where's your ID?" and I was silent. Confused. Not understanding where I actually was. I looked right and left at the concrete posts at my sides. Behind every one of them were soldiers. Palestinians were exiting the waiting line one by one, holding out their IDs. Again she yelled: "Your ID already!!" I stared at her, petrified. A vein stood out in her flushed neck: "Give me your passport!" she screamed in English. Quiet, then another scream: "Your passport!"

I came to my senses and took out my wallet, and out of it, my blue (Israeli) ID. "You're Israeli!" she barked at me. "Idiot, what are you doing here?!" She took my ID and went off to get someone.

I was alone facing the empty concrete block. I looked sideways and back and saw dozens of eyes staring at me. My ears were still ringing with her shout: "You're Israeli, what are you doing . . ." And suddenly I was scared of those stares, afraid of the crowd around me.

Someone behind me yelled in Hebrew: "Why are you messing with them and holding us all up!?"

I looked around for an armed soldier to protect me from them. But the female soldier was already gone and the two soldiers at the side posts did not even lift their eyes from the IDs they were checking. I felt like one of the soldiers at the checkpoint, threatened on every side, but unlike them—naked, exposed, no helmet, no bullet-proof vest, no gun. More moments of fear passed until an older gray-haired soldier came along, in his bullet-proof vest and helmet, his rifle hanging from his neck.

My ID was in his hand and he approached me and asked in a calm voice: "You're from Afula. What are you doing here?"

Before I found a good answer, he asked, "Do you know where you are?" I nodded. "You are not allowed in there. This area is closed to Israelis."

"Closed to Israelis" he tells me, as if I don't know, I thought. Slowly I felt my sense of orientation return. I knew the man facing me was at least forty-five years old and past his reserves-duty days. I knew he was volunteering at the checkpoint to relieve some of the burden the young soldiers were bearing, and to "solve moral issues" as we called it. Indeed, officially he was a soldier like all others and subordinate to the checkpoint commander, but in fact his role was to help the younger soldiers out, using his personal experience and judgment—"humanitarians," such people are called these days.

I too had had humanitarians at the checkpoint. I saw them try, on their first shifts, to be gracious to Palestinians and keep up the appearance of an enlightened occupier, fair and composed. But I also saw them, after their third or fourth shift, begin to lose patience just like all the rest of us. Then exhaustion kicked in, too, and they found themselves tyrannizing people for no reason, grumbling, not listening, even throwing teargas and stun grenades and firing in the air like everyone else.

The man standing in front of me showed me soon enough that he was already in that phase, for before I even answered him, he began yelling at me: "I'll summon the police. Who do you think you are coming here, feeling the big hero, eh?" and immediately began to body-search me roughly. He also summoned another soldier, although I did not resist him at all

I decided I didn't want to complicate matters further and be handed over to the Israeli police. I did what was called for in order to get out of there quickly and quietly. I signaled to him to approach and whispered in his ear: "Listen, I was commander of this checkpoint for a long time." I showed him my reserves-officer card, and said: "Listen, pal, I don't know what I did. I went a bit crazy out here and have come back to see what was going on. Let's keep it quiet so that these guys here"—I pointed discreetly at the Palestinians—"won't slaughter me."

He relented immediately and gave me back my ID, saying: "Go wherever you want."

I began to make my way back among the people in line. My fear of the Palestinians crowded around me returned in full force. I feared every boy and man I passed. Then I saw Yehuda coming with the camera crew and I calmed down again.

In the meantime, they had filmed the construction of the sophisticated terminal that would soon replace the old check-point and lend the occupation an enlightened appearance such as it had never had: a labyrinth of fences erected upon tiled surfaces, and signs welcoming the passers-by and wishing them a safe and pleasant time. The checking staff will be safe inside the perfect sterility of double glazed windows, in front of computer screens, speaking through microphones.

"Don't film here!" the soldiers yelled at the British students who were filming me again as I passed by the line. A moment later the humanitarian showed up again and ran towards us shouting angrily that he was calling the police. He must have felt deceived. The cameraman lowered his camera.

But one of the Palestinians cried out: "Go on, film us! So people can see how we're caged in here, like cattle. Film these shits, go on!"

More soldiers approached. We hurried away from the spot, but then I heard my name loudly called out from the checkpoint. The first question in my mind was: how come a soldier was calling me by my first name and not my last name, as I was called in the army? A fellow got out of the Jeep and came up to shake my hand through the fence: "What are you doing out there? Come through here. It's much easier."

This soldier was from my own village, five years younger than me. When he was in the seventh grade I was his youth movement counselor. He also used to come over to play computer games with my kid brother. My brother put off his own checkpoint hell by one year to do civilian volunteer duty in the *moshav* movement. The soldier suddenly noticed the film crew: "Are you with them?" he asked, grimacing.

"Yes," I answered, and wanted to terminate this meeting. Again I noticed surprised and suspicious looks around me: a moment ago they were looking at a brave journalist, and now they are looking at a friend of a soldier. Once again, I didn't know whom to fear more.

Being at the checkpoint, on its other side, was the most profound psychological transformation I had ever undergone. I recommend it whole-heartedly to any checkpoints soldier whose mind has been scathed.

243

CHAPTER 36

I don't know your name. If I run into you on the street I probably wouldn't even recognize you. I'm not even sure you're alive. Perhaps you died under unnatural circumstances.

We fight inside towns, villages, in your own village, in your backyard. I don't remember what made me come to you in my Jeep. Certainly there was little enough to make my presence attractive. Nor could I now reconstruct my reasons for stopping, getting out and frightening you away. But believe me, I was not looking for your terrified face.

You probably got scared because my gun barrel was pointed directly between your eyes. But you simply don't know, little girl, that when a combatant disembarks from a military vehicle, his gun barrel always follows his gaze. Any combatant could tell you this at the end of basic training: gun barrel follows gaze, gun barrel follows gaze. For what kind of a professional fighter would I be had I seen a good reason to open fire and I had to wait for my rifle to swing into position. Clearly, that fraction of a second could cost the combatant his life. So, with the instinct of a professional fighter, my gun barrel followed my gaze. And my gaze, for just that moment, was turned to you.

I know that no explanation can help here, that I have no chance with you. For me, you are long lost.

I know I am your idea of absolute evil, unless someone even more evil than myself has stolen my title. The truth is that, until now, the possibility has not even crossed my mind: perhaps I am in fact not absolute evil in your eyes but only a transitory evil. Has my place been occupied by anyone else? Was he a soldier, too? And perhaps, God forbid, it was some man who showed you yet another aspect of human evil. And perhaps, who knows, added my form of evil to his own. Forgive me for this terrible thought.

I know the answer myself. There was no one else—I am your absolute evil. I am he. That's why I wanted you to let me tell you a thing or two you don't know about me, things that might make it easier for you to cope with evil. To know that I too, at your age, experienced this kind of absolute evil, the way you did thanks to me. That said, I didn't get to meet the embodiment of wickedness face to face as you did. I only inherited a memory of such a thing. That is why you probably think that my horror is inferior to yours. But know that my idea of absolute evil stretches beyond anything your wildest imagination could conceive. Although I have never seen him myself, his image was present for me, no less sharp and clear as mine was to you.

I did not come all the way here to present justifications to minimize the absolute evil that you see. Why should I? Please listen to me, one moment more: I have rid myself of the absolute evil of my childhood. It no longer exists. And now I have no one to fight. You too can do so if you wish—I would like to teach you how to get rid of absolute evil. Yes, that is what I wanted to do and that is why I walked all the way here.

I parted from it in a way that was especially difficult, by becoming a monster myself. Yes, your absolute evil. Do you understand? That is how I rid myself of that evil of my childhood. You came, appeared in front of me to release me from his grip. I couldn't go on fighting absolute evil as soon as I realized I had turned into such evil myself.

I'm not sure you have to go through this via dolorosa yourself, nor are the political conditions ripe for this yet. Under the present circumstances, all you can do is perhaps blow yourself up in some restaurant or bus, but then your whole story will be over. Perhaps you might try to stab a soldier to death, but then what? Only if you succeed—and you should know your chances for that are slim—only then will you become a small, personal absolute evil for his mother or wife. Perhaps you had better rid yourself of me the way Mahatma Gandhi shrugged off the Brits, or the way the Israelites put Pharaoh behind them.

What am I saying, really? I am losing you again. You are fourteen years old now, perhaps hardly managing your way to school because of all the closures and checkpoints. And I blab away at you about disobedience and liberation.

Okay, so now I shall try to get back to reality and to you. Do listen to me, just another moment.

If you manage to rid yourself of the idea I have become for you, then you win, not only in your conscience but in your reality, in life. If you can look the soldier at the checkpoint in the eye the way that student looked at me, but without the question about evil—"Where do you get all that evil?"—but just look at me as your equal, you win!

You understand? Questions are meant to have answers, but that look—the look of a person struggling to be free—refutes any possibility of answer.

But I have strayed yet again. I want you to be free and happy. Here, I am free and happy today, because I no longer have my Holocaust. I am no longer attached like some tree planted in this cursed earth. I can get away from here, choose a wife of a different people and teach my children another language, never again wield a gun or rule over someone else's will. And all because of you.

If you could steal the Holocaust from all the hundreds of thousands of Israeli soldiers, you'd probably be free along with all of Palestine. But you probably cannot. And please don't be offended. After all this is not your—or my—personal story. It seems that as you grow, your charm and power as a girl who steals the Holocaust dwindle. And anyway, why would all the thousands of Israeli heroes make the pilgrimage to your village to cleanse themselves of their past by grace of a little priestess, a farmer's daughter in a godforsaken village? It's a silly idea . . . I admit, it's silly. I simply came to propose that you forget me the way I forgot the absolute evil that you would never understand.

I just wanted to apologize and didn't know how.
Forgive me.

And don't answer . . . Unfortunately, I cannot answer you. I am busy recovering. Please, do not contact me again.

And again, forgive me.

Your evil,

Noam